P9-DVH-392

DISCARD

PACIFIC
GROVE
PUBLIC
LIBRARY

Presented by

Tricia Lebert

LETTERS
from
LARKSONG

OTHER BOOKS BY DAVID KLINE:

Great Possessions
Scratching the Woodchuck

LETTERS *from* LARKSONG

An Amish Naturalist Explores His Organic Farm

David Kline

Introduction by Wendell Berry

Illustrations by Anna E. Raber

DISCARD

The Wooster Book Company
Wooster Ohio ® 2010

508.771
KLI

Pacific Grove Public Library

The Wooster Book Company

205 West Liberty Street

Wooster, Ohio 44691

Letters from Larksong © 2010 David Kline

"Amish Economics" © 1999 Wendell Berry, from *A Timbered Choir:*
  The Sabbath Poems 1979–1997. Reprinted by permission of Counterpoint LLC

ILLUSTRATIONS © 2010 Anna E. Raber

Material previously appeared in slightly different format in *Farming Magazine:*
  People, Land and Community and in Organic Valley's *Rootstock*

All rights reserved.

SUNNY AUTUMN DAY, George Innes (oil on canvas, 1892)
  Courtesy of The Cleveland Museum of Art

Cover design and foil stamp by Jack Farkas

Printed in the United States of America.

ISBN: 978-1-59098-201-3

LIBRARY OF CONGRESS CATALOGING-IN-PUBLICATION DATA

Kline, David.
   Letters from Larksong / David Kline ; introduction by Wendell Berry ;
illustrations by Anna E. Raber.
         p.   cm.
An Amish naturalist explores his organic farm
including selected columns from Farming magazine.

ISBN 978-1-59098-201-3 (alk. paper)
1. Natural history – Ohio – Anecdotes. 2. Farm life – Ohio – Anecdotes.
3. Kline, David – Homes and haunts – Anecdotes. I. Title.

QH105.O3K555 2010
508.771 – dc22   2010020373

∞ *This book is printed on acid-free paper and the binding is sewn for permanence.*

"Our tools are better than we are, and grow better faster than we do. They suffice to crack the atom, to command the tides. But they do not suffice for the oldest task in human history: to live on a piece of land without spoiling it."

—Aldo Leopold
from *Engineering and Conservation* (1938)

virgin
oak forest

permanent horse
and heifer pasture

LARKSONG FARM
1. _Cliff Swallow colony_
2. _beehives_
3. _vegetable garden_
4. _fruit orchard_
5. _Elderberry bushes_
6. _Savannah Sparrows_
7. _Horned Larks_
8. _Red Fox den_
9. _Eastern Bluebird houses_
10. _Vesper Sparrows_
11. _fencerow of Black Cherry trees_
12. _Serviceberry grove_
13. _Shellbark Hickory trees_
14. _Great Horned Owl's nest_
15. _gigantic Northern Red Oak tree_
16. _Cardinal flowers_
17. _farm pond_
18. _Sugar Maple trees_
19. _old apple orchard_
20. _old Eshleman-farmstead foundation_
21. _American Chestnut tree_
22. _Red-tailed Hawk nest_
23. _Belted Kingfisher colonies_
24. _Northern Rough-winged Swallows_

neighbor's land which we farm

Bobolink field

farm path

Larksong Farm

Harrier field

Table of Contents

LETTERS *from* LARKSONG

Amish Economy

We live by mercy if we live.
To that we have no fit reply
But working well and giving thanks,
Loving God, loving one another,
To keep Creation's neighborhood.

And my friend David Kline told me,
"It falls strangely on Amish ears,
This talk of how you find yourself.
We Amish, after all don't try
To find ourselves. We try to lose
Ourselves"—and thus are lost within.
The found world of sunshine and rain
Where fields are green and then are ripe,
And the people eat together by
The charity of God, who is kind
Even to those who give no thanks.

In morning light, men in dark clothes
Go out among the beasts and fields.
Lest the community be lost
Each day they must work out the bond
Between the goods and their price: the garden
Weeded by sweat is flowerbright;

The wheat shocked in shorn fields, clover
Is growing where wheat grew; the crib
Is golden with the gathered corn,

While in the world of the found selves,
Lost to the sunlit rainy world,
The motor-driven cannot stop.
This is the world where value is
Abstract, and preys on things, and things
Are changed to thoughts that have a price.
Cost + greed – fear = price:
Maury Telleen thus laid it out.
The need to balance greed and fear
Affords no stopping place, no rest
And need increases as we fail.

But now, in summer dusk, a man
Whose hair and beard curl like spring ferns
Sits under the yard trees, at rest
His smallest daughter on his lap.
This is because he rose at dawn,
Cared for his own, helped his neighbors,
Worked much, spent little, kept his peace.

—Wendell Berry
from *A Timbered Choir: The Sabbath Poems 1979–1997*

LETTERS *from* LARKSONG

Introduction

It could be said that *Farming Magazine* sprouted and ripened in the many summer discussions we had while working together in our fields of grain. The consensus was that there was no agricultural publication that supplied the information we desired. That is, information needed by the small-scale diversified farmer who still focused primarily on livestock. The mainstream glossy agribusiness magazines passed us by sometime in the last quarter of the past century. Since more than two dozen of the major agriculture magazines are now owned by Walt Disney, we decided the time was ripe to publish a magazine offering new perspectives and reasons to hope. We are not standing athwart the path of agribusiness yelling, "Stop!" We may goose the ox, not gore him. Rather we aim to offer attractive alternatives to low-profit farming. There are excellent periodicals being published today, but they tend to focus on special issues such as grazing, draft horses, and part-time farming. We wanted a magazine with a wide range of useful and practical information that combined experience, wisdom, and science. We wanted a magazine that radiated hope and the optimism we had for farming.

It has been said that the true test of a sustainable agriculture will be whether we can romance our children into farming. In order for that to occur three things are crucial: 1. Our farms must be profitable; 2. We cannot be overwhelmed by work all the time, and; 3. It must be fun. We at *Farming Magazine* believe in this wisdom.

Albert Camus observed: "All great deeds and great thoughts have a ridiculous beginning." Napoleon likewise noted: "From the sublime to the ridiculous is but a step." We are not claiming greatness or sublimity, but we are very aware of the ridiculous. Here we are, publishing a magazine with no paid staff, no mailing lists, no checking account (yet); we have only a few committed advertisers, a small rented postal box, and a dedicated group of people working to make this dream a reality.

Almost all the editorial work has been done on kitchen and folding tables. Nonetheless, we have had tremendous support from a wide range of dedicated and talented farmers and writers who believe that the magazine is necessary. While our focus will be on the full-time farmer, we are conscious of the "serious part-time farmer." In fact, people who fit the mold of the "serious part-timer" did a considerable part of the writing and artwork in this issue—so we will be kind to them.

John Burroughs said that the thinker "tells" us about a thing, while the artist "gives" us the thing. By making use of both the thinker and the artist we can include a variety of voices—a broad range of opinions. We like the idea of the farm as a work of art. When we make mistakes they are visible for everyone to see, all summer. "Time and nature have a way of painting over a lot of mistakes," Richard Ketchum wrote in *Country Journal*, "There's a lot to be said for a task that broadens your education every day. And next to your own children, what better legacy can you leave posterity than a productive piece of land that delights the eye of the beholder and will help nurture the generations to come?"

We don't know what lies ahead. Our vision, of course, is to publish a widely read and thoroughly enjoyed farming magazine. In future issues we want more departments, more points of view, more perspectives, and more voices. Whatever issues arise, we want *Farming Magazine* to generate more light than heat. Like the red-tailed hawk perched on the edge of its nest in a late-winter snow squall, our hopes are high.

In spite of nighttime temperatures in the teens, the signs of spring are appearing: coltsfoot is blooming, furrows are being turned, and the horned larks are nesting—promises of a new beginning and a new growing season.

(Spring 2001)

Summer

Roadsides sparkle with wild chicory, Queen Anne's lace, Bouncing Bet, and common milkweed. These wildflowers thrive in spite of the drought. And the clover fields abound with butterflies—swallowtails, fritillaries, sulfurs, and monarchs—which flourish on the nectar of the clover blossoms. Dragonflies crisscross the fields hawking for insects. Field corn is tasseling, oats are harvested, and sweet corn is a staple on the dinner table along with fresh blackberries over ice cream. The richness and bounty of the earth is at its finest. I find little wrong with the Dog Days of summer.

A new magazine is a vulnerable endeavor, because its rough edges and the shortcomings of its staff are there for all to see. Like a weedy field. We hope to grub out some of those bull thistles as we travel down the path of publishing *Farming Magazine*.

Our intentions were to have the Summer issue completed by the middle of the season, but we simply got caught up in the busyness of making hay, cultivating corn, eating cherry cobbler, and other necessary work on our farms. (Truthfully, we relaxed too long following the premier issue; lesson well learned.)

People who pay attention to the birth of new magazines say the second issue is the one to watch. Any numbskull, they say, can come up with a good first copy if they work hard enough. The issues that follow will show whether there is meat on the skeleton of the publication.

We are experiencing our worst drought since 1988 in this part of Ohio and as we're waiting for rain, we listen to the halting screams of young redtails high in the heated summer sky and realize that things could be a lot worse.

(2001)

The Monarch

We are grazing second-crop hayfields and not much green is left in the searing heat, except a scattering of common milkweeds, which the Jerseys refuse to eat. When I moved the fence yesterday, I checked one of the milkweeds and found what I hoped to find, a young monarch butterfly caterpillar feeding on the underside of a leaf.

The larva was only half an inch long and as big around as an uncooked strand of spaghetti. But it was there and that was good news to me. After researchers at Cornell University found that the pollen of a genetically engineered strain of field corn, the so-called Bt corn, killed monarch caterpillars, I have worried that fewer monarchs will brighten our summers.

Ever since genetic engineering became the *Wunderkind* of the agricultural corporate giants, there has been a growing concern that incidents such as the monarch killing will become more prevalent. When Linda Rayor and her Cornell colleagues, Maureen Carter and John Losey, published their article, "Transgenic Pollen Harms Monarch Larvae," in the British scientific journal, *Nature*, I wasn't surprised. After watching a generation of farmers, including my dad, suffer from the ravages of Parkinson's disease; a generation of farmers active in the 1940s and 50s who were advised by agricultural experts to spray their clover fields with the insecticide heptachlor (closely related to DDT) to kill spittlebugs; it takes more than the Cornell report to shock me. Perhaps I'm too cynical, but I was expecting something along this line. Now we wait for the other shoe to drop. I'm afraid the empire has the feet of a millipede and many shoes will have to drop before heads will be raised in attention.

Bt corn came about by inserting the gene of the soil bacterium *Bacillus thuringienis* into the corn's genetic code, tricking the corn to produce its own Bt bacterium. Bt secretes a protein, that when eaten by the larvae of many different kinds of butterflies and moths, rots their gut and they die. Organic vegetable growers, Dipel for one, have used Bt with especially good results on cole crops for many years. However, it wasn't used over the hundreds of thousands of acres that Bt corn is grown.

Corn producing its own insecticide was considered a victory in controlling the European corn borer, a pest found where corn is grown year after year in the same field. In regions like ours, where most row crops are rotated annually, the corn borer is no pest, hence no Bt corn is planted and monarch caterpillars can feed on milkweeds without harm.

Following the Cornell report, the biotech industry roared like a gored bull and quickly and vigorously responded with press releases, mostly stupid ones, such as monarchs don't breed during the time corn is pollinating (ours do), and that milkweeds don't grow next to cornfields. As a result of the lowly monarch, three biotech giants: Monsanto Company, Novartis AG of Switzerland, and Pioneer Hi-Bred of Dupont Company, formed a slick consortium, the Agricultural Biotechnology Stewardship Working Group (ABSWG). This group now runs ads in many of the major (non-farm, of course) magazines, showing a smiling farmer, and telling us we're all far better off with biotechnology. I wonder whether they asked the monarchs in our hayfield?

The first monarch of the year arrived here on June 3rd, and then I didn't see another one for two weeks. It wasn't until well into summer, when our local broods began emerging, that monarchs became a common sight in our garden and fields, and I breathed a sigh of relief. The late summer hatch of monarchs throughout the Midwest is crucial to their survival, because this is the brood that migrates the long perilous journey to the Sierra Madre Oriental in Mexico.

The monarchs that fly to our farm in June are likely the grandchildren of those that migrated to Mexico the previous autumn. No monarch ever makes the round-trip flight. When I read, sometime in the 1970s, in *National Geographic* that the Canadian naturalist, Fred Urquhart, had found the wintering grounds of the eastern race of the monarch butterfly in the mountains of Mexico, it was hard to believe that such a fragile creature could fly two thousand miles!

Whenever I see a monarch winging across our fields in late summer, always toward the southwest and Mexico and into the prevailing winds, I pause in admiration. Then I wonder where the monarch is that I moved from the leaf on the milkweed in the pasture to the milkweed by the cornfield? I wish it well.

Fall

We think of spring as the miracle, the rebirth, to the abundance of the growing season. Autumn seems more like closure, the departure of something rich and beautiful. But if we look closely, autumn is as miraculous as spring—the bounty of summer is now enclosed in the seed. Seeds that now are dispersing to fertile ground to wait out the long cold time of winter before again greening the earth.

Milkweed pods are opening and their downy seeds are sown by the wind, burrs and stickems hitch rides on fur and denim, witch hazel's tough pods explode and shoot their seeds up to thirty-five feet from the parent tree, acorns and hickory nuts are carried and planted by animals, the corn we harvest and store for humans and animals.

It is the rustle of drying corn leaves as much as anything that reminds us of the change as the last monarch pitches and yaws across the fields and the first rough-legged hawk down from the Arctic gets a cold shoulder from the local flock of crows.

It has been said that there is nothing like an average year. An average is when extremes are balanced, an equalization of opposites. This growing season will give balance to an exceptionally wet year—most of us non-irrigating farmers in this part of the country were hurt by the summer's drought. I cannot recall a year that we kept our eyes focused so much on the western horizon, searching for promising thunderheads.

In all our years of dairy farming, our hay supply has never been this low. Most of our second and subsequent crops of hay were needed for pasture. We were fortunate that by grazing the hay fields we were then spared from feeding stored hay. I have an aversion to feeding dry hay during the grazing season. Hay is for winter feeding. Should the temperatures remain moderate, the late rains will help to extend the pasture season into late November.

The drought also brought with it unusually high incidents of bloat in dairy cows. A number of dairy farmers I talked to lost one or more cows to the legume-caused killer. We had one panic-stricken evening when almost half our herd was bloated from ladino. We lost two, Ivana and Linda.

Milk prices, partly because of the drought in parts of the eastern dairy belt, were good. It all averages out, I guess.

On August 9 the drought was partially broken when two severe thunderstorms gave us two and a half inches of rain. For about three hours there was constant lightning and thunder. Unfortunately, one of those powerful strokes of lightning smashed into our neighbor's barn and within minutes the barn was engulfed in flames.

From out of the ashes of disaster often arise the finest and greatest efforts of labor and love in a community and a nation.

When the last leaves are on the compost pile and the woodpile stacked high, may your holiday season be warm and blessed.

(2001)

The Bees

The Pedigree of Honey
Does not concern the Bee—
A Clover, any time, to him,
Is Aristocracy—

—Emily Dickinson

I had a pleasant surprise the other week. I opened the beehive and discovered every frame filled to the edges with clover and locust blossom honey. Likewise, the brood chamber frames were overflowing with young bees—from eggs to sealed brood—an indication of an excellent queen along with plenty of pollen and nectar. Amid all the bad news on disappearing bees worldwide, I was hesitant to check the bees in fear of what I would find. With joy I gave the bees another super of drawn comb to fill with clover nectar.

Because of the early summer drought, we grazed all of our second cutting hay and I had some time on my hands. So the following week, I set up the archaic two-frame A.I. Root honey extractor in the basement, fired up the capping melter, and set out to steal the two supers of honey from the bees. Stuffing the bee smoker with baler twine and lighting it, I cracked the hive lid and gave the bees a few puffs of sisal smoke. Waiting a few moments for the bees to move lower into the hive, I removed the cover and inner cover and to my amazement found the bees had already filled the new super with thirty pounds of white clover honey. All in a week's time!

While I "manage" the honeybees to work for us, they still are not domesticated and remain wild animals. (Our Jersey bull sometimes pretends he's a wild animal, but he's not). When the bees bring the nectar into the hive, it is too high in water content to be honey. The bees then have to evaporate the moisture from the nectar to turn it into honey. This is done by a number of bees, maybe a hundred, fanning their wings at 250 beats per second at the hive entrance, which forces air up through the frames and the nectar becomes honey. Once the honey is "right," the hive bees cap and seal it with wax.

But honey is more than nectar alone. The naturalist John Burroughs wrote in *Wake-robin* in 1895,

> Most persons think the bee gets honey from the flowers, but she does not: honey is a product of the bee; it is nectar of the flowers with the bee added. What the bee gets from the flower is sweet water; this she puts through a process of her own and imparts to it her quality; she reduces the water and adds to it a minute drop of formic acid. It is this drop of herself that gives the delicious sting to her sweet. The bee is therefore the type of the poet, the true artist. Her product always reflects her environment, and it reflects something her environment knows not of. We taste the clover, the thyme, the linden, the sumac, and we also taste something that has its source in none of these flowers.

Now instead of two supers, my daughter Ann and I spun out three supers and eight gallons of likely the finest honey I've seen in my thirty-some years of keeping honeybees.

I do know that I have never extracted fresher honey – from nectar to table in eight days. The nice part is that we now have eight gallons of food that will never spoil, using almost no fossil fuel – perhaps a pint of camping gas in the old Coleman camp stove to heat the water in the capping melter. The Coleman I picked up free from the no-sale wagon following the spring Mt. Hope Machinery Auction. Renita usually charges a dollar for those unsold items, but in her kindness she gave me the heater. I will give her honey in exchange. My wife will use the beeswax from the cappings to make Christmas candles for the family and the faint aroma of the bee and summer will linger all the way through the holiday season.

I returned the three extracted supers to the hive giving what I hoped was ample space for honey storage for the next six weeks, or until the fall honey flow. The fall honey from goldenrod and aster tends to be dark and of a stronger flavor. The bees don't mind eating that honey during the cold months. Yesterday, Joseph the bee inspector stopped to check the colony for foulbrood, mites, hive beetles, or problems bees encounter. His report was that the bees are in excellent condition. He added that the top super is already filled with new honey and that the queen is doing her job too well and has moved into the other two honey supers and is filling them with brood.

That means I have to smoke her down into the brood chambers and place a queen excluder between her and the honey supers. The bees would eventually force her down and fill the frames, after the brood has hatched, with fall honey. I don't want to wait for that and miss all the white clover honey. The good queen in the hive, along with several frames of sealed brood and honey, was brought to me by Joseph a year ago when he inspected our colony and found them queenless. The bees had swarmed and apparently something happened to the young queen. A colony of bees without a queen is doomed.

For seventy-five dollars Joseph rescued our colony. A bargain. He told me the other day that the queen was from a wild swarm. For many centuries, beekeepers thought the queen was king of the colony. It wasn't until the 1600s that it was discovered the "king" had ovaries and is the mother of all the bees. So thanks to the queen and her court, we have honey and, because of their pollination efforts, Macintosh apple sauce for the winter months.

Few things can compare with a piece of fresh wheat bread still warm from the oven spread with butter and covered with white clover honey dripping off the sides. What I then like to add is a slice of sun-ripened tomato, zaftig with the goodness of summer, a touch of salt, and I've got a feast that the upscale New York eateries have a tough time to match.

Winter

Here we are a week from the winter solstice and the weather seems like early October. Is this bad weather? My body and the white-footed mice in the woodpile love it, but my mind tells me something is awry. Only a few times in past years have we grazed this late in the season and then it was only after enduring several periods of really foul weather in late October and November. This year it has been almost balmy all through the autumn season. And with our pastures having a two-month rest in the middle of the summer, they paid us back this fall. The grasses are still growing. Wild mustard and dandelions are blooming (I have seen dandelion bloom in every month of the year but never before have I seen them develop into seed heads in December), lilacs and forsythias are showing new growth, and the cat had kittens. Perhaps Wes Jackson is correct in suggesting that before long, strawberries will be grown on Baffin Island.

Long and leisurely autumns are nice in that the transition to winter feeding is gradual. It gets the cows acclimated to stored feed and the drop in production isn't so drastic. We still have fall-seeded oats (a winter cover crop in the three acres where corn was removed for silage) that could be grazed but I think we'll call it the end of the grazing season, and in a few weeks the year will end.

The writer William Kittredge defines sacred as those things we cannot do without. The human-wrought catastrophes of late summer made us aware how many things we were taking for granted, and how many things that we can do without. At the end of the millennium two years ago, the national news magazines (*Time*, *Newsweek*, et al) tried to outdo each other with special issues on what the next century will offer us in the way of the good life; the focus was primarily on technological gizmos. I have forgotten most of the wonders they visualized, but many were things we can do without, things that would not meet Kittredge's definition of sacred.

What really caught my attention, or rather what was missing in their glowing prophecies: food was not mentioned. Apparently food will always be abundant and as close as the supermarket. No need for further discussion. One economist even suggested that the United States should quit producing food and import it. We should become solely an information-entertainment-dispensing nation, he claimed. I reckon the Argentines would go for that right now.

I believe that the quality of life begins on the dinner plate. Food is something we cannot do without and live. Those of us living on agriculturally productive land are fortunate. Not only can we produce food for our livelihood, we can grow food for our families and ourselves. At mealtime we often look at the food on the table and see how much was grown on our farm—practically all of it except the salt and pepper and my favorite habanero pepper sauce.

(2001)

Spring

Of all the season changes, I must confess, spring is my favorite. Those pleasingly warm March days when coats are pitched and shirtsleeves rolled up are hard to beat. The dooryard robins are back, coltsfoot is blooming, the horned larks are nesting, and our eastern meadowlarks are singing, "Spring of the year is here."

Even though our winter was mild, spring is still a treat, like the warm embrace of a friend who spent the winter in Florida. This is the time of the year when I think we should travel at the speed of the sun—like the spring, the sun is moving north about fifteen miles a day. That is the distance I plow in a day. Walking all day in a furrow of winter-cooled soil that releases its rich, earthy aroma to proclaim the rebirth of another growing season is savoring spring to the dregs.

Here in the field, life slows down to the speed of nature. Almost daily new birds arrive in the fields—American pipits, Savannah and vesper sparrows, and redwings. Turkey vultures and red-tailed hawks soar and search for a meal. Sometimes surprises drop at my feet—a lost Crescent wrench that was a wedding gift. Last year a nice two-inch-long arrowhead was just waiting to be picked up. Stone tools and flint points I find tell me that there were a people, a culture, here before us that must have awaited the return of the sun and warmth and migrating waterfowl and food. A people who lived and traveled lightly on the land and left behind only enduring reminders of what they used to gather food. Every time I find a piece of their handwork, be it a stone, flint, or slate ornament, I hold it in my hand and try to visualize the last human to touch it before me. Hopewell? Iroquois? Shawnee? Erie? Delaware?

If "to plow is to pray," as indeed it may be, sowing the seed is an act of faith. We put our trust in the miracle of the seed and good soil and rain and sunshine. If all goes well, harvest time will come, but for now I'm perfectly contented to have and hold spring and its beauty, surprises, and promises of grasses and color.

Sometimes, we simply get behind. You should see the manure pile behind the barn waiting to be spread. I tell the neighbors it's being composted—manure, like humans, gets better with age.

May all your seeds sprout and flourish.

(2002)

Dragonflies

I have always admired the flight skills of dragonflies, along with their fearlessness in wandering far from streams and marshes. The other day, while I was mowing hay, green darners and twelve-spotted skimmers were hunting and hawking for insects over the field. They seemed unmindful of the dozens of insect-hunting swallows that wheeled around them. The dragonflies, like the swallows, have voracious appetites for flying insects, but they evaded the hungry birds as easily as houseflies dodge the swatter.

In some ways the green darners seem more like birds than the insects they are. Unlike the swallows, which catch their prey with their bills, the dragonflies capture theirs with their forward-thrusting spiny legs that form a basketlike net. Flying at full speed, they scoop the insects out of the air. Once caught, the prey is transferred to the dragonfly's mouth with its front two legs. Dragonflies are so well adapted for flight—they can hover and wheel, shoot straight up, fly backward and dart sideways at full speed—that their legs are almost useless for walking. They are either flying or perched; like a switch, on or off.

There are 450 species of dragonflies and damselflies in North America. Damselflies are more slender and delicate than the dragonflies, and when at rest they fold their wings together above their bodies. Around 125 have been recorded in Northeast Ohio, with eighty of those being dragonflies.

Almost as charming as the antics of the dragonflies, are their names. When the common names were given to these big and beautiful insects, poets must have been offering suggestions. When we enter wetlands and bogs in the heat of summer, we may encounter Illinois River cruisers, smoky shadowdragons, cherry-faced meadowhawks, sphagnum sprites, mocha emeralds, or perhaps Laura's clubtail.

The common green darner is the largest and fastest-flying dragonfly here in the Central Highlands of Ohio. Sue Hubbell writes in her book *Broadsides from the Other Orders* that darners have been clocked at speeds up to sixty mph. Appearing in mid-April, the darners are around until late October and then tend to migrate southward to warmer hunting grounds.

Dragonflies begin their lives in water as ferocious predators. In this stage, the nymphs, or naiads, capture insects, tadpoles, and even fingerling fish. The naiads are highly beneficial predators because they feed primarily on mosquito larvae—those wigglers that rise to the surface of the water troughs for air and then wiggle back down as you dip out water. Especially now that mosquito-borne West Nile Disease is so prevalent, underwater predators are crucial in helping control the sickness.

After one or two years of aquatic life and living through ten to fifteen molts, the naiad crawls out of the water, and clinging to some solid support, its skin splits along the top of the thorax and an adult dragonfly emerges. Should the dragonfly lose its grip and drop into the water, it would drown. It is now an air-breathing creature. For a few hours after emerging, the dragonfly rests to give its wings time to dry and harden. Once the process, which entomologists call tanning, is completed, the dragonfly begins its life as an airborne predator. It now hunts flying mosquitoes.

Dragonflies will venture far from water to hunt, but they will return to ponds and streams and marshes to mate and lay their eggs. It is around wetlands where the greatest varieties of dragonflies are found. Last summer, a friend and I went searching for the Indian village called Killbuck's Town. Supposedly, some of the treaties signed by William Penn were kept in this town. (Not that we hoped to find them.) Old maps show the village to have been in a number of locations. But Andy, who thinks like a Native American, came to the logical conclusion that the town was on the upland, west of the Killbuck and the fording place where William Crawford crossed with his ill-fated army.

So we went looking, hoping to unravel the mystery in the high heat and humidity of last year's drought. What we had not anticipated was the jungle of multiflora roses. Occasionally crawling on hands and knees and following animal trails, we found no concrete proof of Chief Killbuck's town, but we did find several clearings bulldozed and leveled for oil wells that never materialized. In these clearings devoid of topsoil, a colorful display of acid-loving late summer wildflowers were in bloom – goldenrods, blue vervain, boneset, mints, and wingstem. And flying and flitting among those wildflowers was the grandest assortment of dragonflies and damselflies I have ever seen.

These human-created meadows are only a short distance from hundreds of acres of swamplands; a perfect place for order *Odonata*. There were the ubiquitous darners and there were skimmers and baskettails and bluets and whitefaces – for most of them I had no names.

For many years there were no good field guides for dragonflies because they weren't glamour species like birds and butterflies. Now, at last (2002), a new field guide has been published by Larry Rosche called *Dragonflies and Damselflies of Northeast Ohio* (Cleveland Museum of Natural History). Ian Adams gave me a copy and it is excellent. I shall return to the hillside meadows with close-focusing binoculars and field guide in hand.

Summer

This is the time of the year when the sun reaches its zenith and the season of summer begins; a season so generous that it gives us fifteen-hour days to harvest its abundance. Summer is a time for getting things done. It is also vacation time for those who need to escape to somewhere else to avoid getting things done.

Vacation is from the Latin root *vac*–"empty"–the words vacation and vacuum are near kin. It is a shame to waste the longest days of the year doing what evenings and Sundays are for ... resting. Last winter at one of our local grazing seminars, a speaker from Ireland told this story, "A feed salesman paid a visit to an Irish farmer and finding him a hard-sell, offered this advice, 'You should milk twice as many cows as you're milking now. Then you'd generate enough income that you could afford a two-week holiday every year.' After a few moments of thought the farmer replied, 'You mean to tell me that I should kill myself fifty weeks out of the year to take two weeks off? No thanks. I'm on holiday fifty-two weeks out of the year.'"

On a more somber note, the February 2002 issue of *Harper's Magazine* had an excellent article by Barry Commoner (some of us remember him from *Common Cause*) titled "Unraveling the DNA Myth: The Spurious Foundation of Genetic Engineering." Commoner, who is senior scientist at the Center for the Biology of Natural Systems at Queens College, City University of New York, unveils many of the fallacies and dangers of genetic engineering, particularly in agriculture. With the completion of the three-billion dollar Human Genome Project in 2001, one of the largest and most highly publicized scientific undertakings of our time, and the discovery that instead of the one-hundred thousand or more genes predicted by the estimated number of human proteins, the gene count was only thirty thousand. By comparison, a mustard-like weed has twenty-six thousand genes. The surprising result of the project shows that genetic manipulation is much more complex than commonly believed.

Commoner points out that the genetic engineers of food crops placed all their bets on a forty-year-old and outdated scientific theory called the "central dogma." This is a theory used in declaring that the genetic modification of food crops is "specific, precise, and predictable" and therefore safe. For instance, the outcome of transferring a DNA gene between species such as the bacterial gene (Bt) into a corn plant is expected to be as predictable as the result of a corporate takeover: what the workers do will be determined precisely by what the new top management tells them to do.

Almost seventy percent of the soybeans and cotton, and twenty-six percent of the corn grown in this country are genetically modified. Given the failure of the central dogma, the genetically engineered crops now being grown represent a massive uncontrolled experiment whose outcome is inherently unpredictable. The results could be catastrophic.

We dairy farmers are already seeing some catastrophic results. During last year's drought, many of us here in this region ran out of grain. Although we farm organically, we aren't selling our milk as organic, so we bought grain from the conventional market and promptly lost a cow. The veterinarian diagnosed it as severe acidosis caused by overfeeding of grains. This was not the case. I blame the genetically defiled grains and soybeans. We, and other dairy farmers with similar problems, had become a part of that uncontrolled experiment.

Commoner concludes, "Why, then, has the central dogma continued to stand? To some degree the theory has been protected from criticism by a device more common to religion than science: dissent, or merely the discovery of a discordant fact, is a punishable offense, a heresy that might easily lead to professional ostracism

... what the public fears is not experimental science but the fundamentally irrational decision to let the experiment out of the laboratory into the real world before we truly understand it."

The local feed mill supplies their customers who wait in line with salted-in-the-shell peanuts. While standing in line, shelling peanuts, and listening to farmer news, I saw a bumper sticker: "We Back Biotech" (from Novartis, a biotech company). It was pasted to the trash barrel where we tossed our peanut shells.

(2002)

Why Organic?

It was time for a break during the afternoon of hay baling. Stopping everything in the shade of the hickory, wild cherry, and serviceberry trees along the fenceline, mow crew and field crew stretched out in the pleasant shade. We were enjoying our refreshments, when someone noticed a polyphemus moth in last year's leaf litter near the fence. Nearly emerged from its silken cocoon, the moth was "tanning" (curing) his wings, which were a good five inches across. The moth was brownish yellow with eyespots on both forewings and hindwings and the wings were edged along the back with a band of rich ochre. It was perfect in every way.

Sometimes a desire for a natural solution to a vexing problem can take a wrong turn and end up doing more harm than good. Such has been the case with the giant silk moths, like the polyphemus we admired.

Ever since an amateur scientist named Étienne Léopold Trouvelot inadvertently released gypsy moths from his Massachusetts home in 1869, and staked his claim to entomological infamy, a search has been on for a natural control for the imported forest-damaging moths. Starting in 1906 scientists began releasing a parasitic tachinid fly, *Compsilura concinnata*, to try to keep the runaway moths in check.

The parasitic fly resembles the familiar housefly but has more hair. Unlike the parasitic ichneumon wasps, which often parasitize only one host species, this imported fly is a generalist and particularly destructive, since it attacks dozens of species of moths, including the beautiful giant silk moths such as the polyphemus, luna, cecropia, and promethea.

As the gypsy moth migrated west out of New England, the tachinid fly followed and the silk moth populations plummeted. Each female fly carries about two hundred eggs. When she spots a meaty caterpillar, she hatches one egg in her oviduct and then injects the larva directly into her victim. One fly can take out an entire fencerow of silk moth larvae. Where there could be found scores of pendulum-like promethea moth cocoons swinging from the twigs of wild cherry and sassafras sprouts along fencelines in decades past, today there are only a few, or more likely none. Entomologists quit releasing the destructive parasitic fly in 1986, but it was too late to undo the damage.

While such extensive harm may occur from misguided attempts at biocontrolling pests, what we see on our organically managed farm is just the opposite. I like to think that the tachinid fly about to parasitize the polyphemus moth larva last year was eaten by one of the flycatchers or yellow warblers common along the fencerow. The larva then lived to spin itself into a cocoon and emerge almost a year later, for our viewing pleasure.

I am by nature an optimist and am convinced that by working with nature, instead of fighting against it, we will be rewarded far beyond our expectations.

The other evening, I had the privilege of walking across our farm with a skeptic. He was a young dairy farmer from a southern state where the soil is red and its organic matter low. Organic farming just will not work, he claimed. And then the questions came:

Do you soil test? What is your base saturation? Your cation exchange capacity? What about starter fertilizer? Nitrogen?

No, I said, we haven't taken soil samples for at least ten years. That was when the organic researchers at The Ohio State University did some comparison studies on our farm and we got free soil testing out of their work. I tried to explain that my philosophy on farming may partly be a result from reading Thoreau. But before taking Thoreau's advice, I had taken a long detour and learned some hard lessons on soils and husbandry.

After my wife and I took over the farm and dairy in the late 1960s, I signed up with a reputable soil testing and consulting laboratory. I soon discovered that the view from their offices differed considerably from my dad's feet-on-the-soil vision. Dad had always practiced the traditional four-year rotation and every fourth year when the field went to wheat, we applied two tons of high-calcium lime. The field going into corn got the bulk of the barn manure. It worked well. Clover and alfalfa flourished and so did the other crops. Our third and fourth cuttings of hay were grazed by the herd of Guernseys.

Soon I was poring over soil sample reports and learned to understand at least part of the complicated terminology. No, field one that went to wheat in September did not need lime, which was nice. For ten years we needed no lime. No compacted lime truck tracks to harrow out. Soon we bought a fertilizer drill and a spinner spreader. Rock phosphate and Sul-Po-Mag and cake mix blends were spread and Dad merely smiled. He did not have to tell me that life was getting to be a lot more complicated and our fields were dwindling in fertility. The soil worked harder from the lack of calcium.

Then I read Thoreau, took Henry's counsel of "Simplify, simplify" to heart and applied it to our farm and learned to live close to nature. I got rid of the fertilizer drill and sent the spinner spreader with the scrap and recycle man.

This is what I learned, I said. Take time to turn now and then and watch the soil crumble as it furls away from the plow, as good soil should. Take a handful of soil, feel its tilth and smell and taste its richness. Count earthworms and observe dung beetles and watch butterflies. Get to know every foot of your farm; every granite boulder; every species of bird, local and migratory. Learn to recognize the wild mammals and their tracks and habits. Don't plant the sweet corn near the woods or shelter the pullets too close to the red-tailed hawks' nest. Study the growing plants. Are they thriving or sickly? Become familiar with the weeds. They have a story to tell.

I explained to my southern friend that the weeds are my soil report and we are back to using only high-calcium lime, manure, and legumes—a practice I never should have left. I needed that ten-year span of hard-earned lessons to dampen my hubris. Of course, I said, I may have an unfair advantage in that this farm has been traditionally-farmed for ninety years and has no soil compaction. The farm is very forgiving of mistakes I make.

When we certified for the first time, the certifier and I walked across the fields and I told him the story of the farm. He carried a two-foot long soil probe to check for soil compaction and soil quality. He never used it. He could feel the life and tilth through his feet. That spoke well for Dad's wisdom and farming methods.

As we watched the polyphemus moth, he pumped his wings like a weight-lifter and then appeared ready for flight. By nightfall, the moth likely tuned his antennae to the pheromones of a female at the far end of the field by the woods, and I hope next year there will be more moths along the fencerow for the haying crew to enjoy.

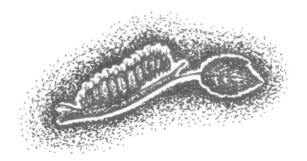

Fall

We are nearing the end of another summer in which we spent a lot of time waiting for rain. It was almost a rerun of the drought of 2001. There were some differences though … last year it was dry and cool during the heart of the summer, daytime temperatures in the lower to mid eighties. This year it was dry and hot with day after day of ninety degrees. One of the first things I do in the morning is check the outside temperature. The rule of thumb is that if the thermometer reads seventy degrees at 5:00 A.M. it will hit ninety by early afternoon. This summer the early morning temperature could be sixty degrees and it would still soar into the nineties by mid-afternoon. Why? The neighborhood theory is that the earth is simply so warm from all the heat that normal rules don't apply anymore.

We were fortunate to have had all the early spring rains we did because that replenished the springs and ground water. All summer the springs kept purling along. On the negative side this year is the low milk price. Last year, along with the cooler temperatures, the price of milk was pretty good. Low milk prices coupled with high hay prices is a tough match for dairy farmers. On the positive side, if we survive this summer, we have been conditioned for the long haul.

Recently I have been reading a book titled *The Fourth Turning: An American Prophecy* (1997). The authors, William Straus and Neil Howe, point out that over the past five centuries, Anglo-American society has entered a new era—a new turning—every two decades or so. Turnings come in cycles of four; each cycle spanning the length of a long human life, about eighty years. According to their view we are now about to enter a Fourth Turning; a crisis period similar to the one our parents and grandparents experienced during the 1930s and into the 1940s. The Roaring Twenties were

followed by the stock market crash, the Depression and drought years. Franklin Delano Roosevelt said in his first inaugural address in 1933, "The money changers have fled from their high seats in the temple of our civilization." Sounds like the present decade.

My parents started farming in 1929. As Dad used to say, "Just as things started to roll … the wrong direction." For years he would caution me not to plant the corn too heavily, "Because if it doesn't rain, you won't get anything." Back then I would chuckle to myself over his cautious attitude. Now I know what he meant. Right now it's possible to find fields of corn planted, as Dad would say, "as thick as the hair on a dog," that have no ears of grain. And if the farmer has no livestock to graze the corn or to eat it ensiled, it's a lost crop.

That brings me to a similar but different topic. It does matter what we eat, where it comes from, and the quality of the food. Statistics show we are a nation of overweight people, and consumers are becoming softer and flabbier as they increase in size. Our vegetables are growing larger and prettier and more tasteless. The commercially produced cantaloupes I have eaten this summer are bigger and much firmer than earlier varieties and unfortunately taste like orange cucumbers.

(2002)

White Oak

Two years ago a severe thunderstorm blew down a large white oak in our woods. On its way down, another oak was sideswiped and broken off twenty feet up. As this summer's work on the farm waned, we decided it was time to make order out of the tangled mess. We cut four saw logs; one seventeen feet long, two eight, and one ten-footer. The next step was getting them out of the woods, since the only way out was up a fairly steep and long slope.

Our son-in-law was up to the challenge. Borrowing a neighbor's log trailer, he hitched four horses—two in front of two and took those good oaks up that slope and the half mile to the road. The four-horse team was almost maxed out on the seventeen-footer, but Big Hank gave it some extra thrust and the trailer and log shot up over the hill and on to the road.

From the road, the logs were taken to a friend's sawmill where they will be sawn into boards and planks and beams needed here on the farm. The pump platform covering the top of our eighteen-foot-deep, hand-dug well is sagging and needs to be replaced before someone disappears into its depths. The oak will supply the material.

All my growing up years, my dad had a sawmill. Whenever we needed a building on the farm, we would go to the woods and check out the oaks. Dad would select one and we would cut it down. After wrangling the big logs up to the little mill, we soon had our lumber for the corncrib, or barn addition, ready to go.

Although our woods had a nice number of virgin white and red oaks, Dad sold very few because he believed they were more important to use as needed on the farm and for their aesthetic value and for dens and food for squirrels and other mammals. He did sell two white oaks, sometime in the 1930s, to British shipwrights that squared two feet at forty feet from the stump. The forty-foot logs were used for keel beams in ships. My guess is that the huge white oaks were used to build wooden sailing vessels since only the finest white oaks were acceptable to British shipwrights. When I see pictures of those tall sailing ships, I like to think that oak from our farm may be in their structure. Many oaks went into building those tall ships. The American frigate *Constitution* took fifteen hundred trees.

I did not realize how old the white oaks in our woods were until several years ago, when a class of students took borings from some of the oaks and then counted the growth rings. One tree dated back well into the 1600s. Most of the others started growing in the 1700s.

Across Europe and North America people built their civilization out of oak. Many of the material necessities for settled human life came from the oak tree.

Here in the eastern edge of the Corn Belt and on the western fringe of the Allegany Plateau, oak is a part of our everyday lives. Besides our barns, which are almost solid oak, we haul our grain in wagons resting on oak beams, I climb up oak rungs to the hay mow—in our houses we sleep on bed frames of oak, we walk on oak, we kneel on oak, sit on oak, eat from the top of oak, store our cider inside oak barrels.

Before the forklift, pallets, and 55-gallon steel drums displaced the need for oak barrels (except for the ageing of spirits, wines, and Worcestershire sauce) much of the shipped cargo was transported in oak. Barrels contained anything from nails, butter, and bourbon, to pickled herring in quantities up to half a ton. A barrel could be easily rolled down a ship's deck or dockside by merely nudging either end to change the direction of its roll and then could be safely stacked, five high, for transport.

A well-made oak barrel can also withstand tremendous pressure, up to thirty pounds per square inch – about the same as an automobile tire. I know. A few years ago, we needed a new cider barrel and when I took our last apples of the fall to the local cider press, I bought a thirty-gallon oak barrel from him and he filled it with sweet cider.

For bringing the cider home and getting it into the cellar, I tapped the wooden stopper tightly into the bunghole on the side of the barrel. Once safely in the cellar, I set it on end with intentions of boring a hole and inserting a wooden spigot for easy access to the cask's sweet contents.

As so often happens on a farm, a few days slipped into several weeks before my mind returned to the cider in the cellar. I got a spigot from Lehman's and after the evening milking, I proceeded with the hand brace to bore a hole through the end of the barrel. I wanted to be careful that no wood chips fell into the cider.

My worries about wood chips in the cider were unwarranted. The instant the bit broke through the oak, an explosion of cider erupted, hitting me square in the face, and as I ducked away, continued to shoot to the joists and ceiling overhead for what seemed an awfully long time. I finally got the spigot pounded into the hole and the geyser stopped. I surveyed the mess and decided that the taste of the Northern Spy/Jonathon/Grimes Golden blend of apples wasn't too bad. Not bad at all.

It has been said that working with oak occupies the brain, the hand, and the emotions, all at the same time. Years ago Dad and I had rolled our oak logs onto the carriage of the sawmill with cant hooks. He operated the controls and the set; I carried the slabs up the pile and then stacked the boards. I was the off-bearer. Being downwind, I would catch the fresh fragrance of the oak wood as the big saw blade bit into the log and sliced off boards.

When we bring home the lumber from my friend's mill, the smell of the rough-sawn wood will rekindle my emotions and renew my love and appreciation for good oak.

Winter

I'm writing a bit later in the season, but nevertheless it is still officially autumn and the wind is howling and the snow is swirling around the corners of the house. Here, within four feet of the living room woodstove, I'm as comfortable as the white-footed mouse deep within the woodpile in its nest of milkweed down and soft grasses.

I have yet to find a more comfortable wintertime heat than wood. (I haven't tried Tucson). Right now I'm warmed by seasoned ash and cherry. Today, I scouted our woods to see what is available for the winter (I'm not as diligent as Gene Logsdon, who cuts his wood a year in advance; I'm more of a deadwood-cutter and work only a month or two ahead). Two wind-blown ash trees should heat the house for six weeks; a large sugar maple that succumbed to old age will add another month; a black gum down, but unsplittable, with a number of nice dead red elms and several small oaks brings us to April.

I was anticipating a long mild Indian-summery autumn on account of the unusually warm summer. The earth was heated like soapstone, the waters of Lake Erie were above normal temperatures, and so we were set for grazing into December. But I was wrong. By mid-October the jet stream slipped to the south of us and the door to Canada's frigid air was opened. If this weather continues, there will be ice-skating, and possibly ice-cutting, before Christmas, and then we'll see whether the local weather prophet who insists that "if a man can walk on the ice before Christmas, a dog can't afterward," is right. The skaters hope he's wrong.

To get back to my reconnoitering in the woods for firewood – of course I was pleased to see the ample supply of firewood, but I was also delighted to see the abundance of birds and mammals, and their signs. Tracks of fox squirrels and cottontail rabbits were everywhere. Several red fox were around during the night, their tracks meandering through the meadow. Our resident birds – chickadees, titmice, and cardinals are doing well. And so are the woodpeckers. I saw a red-headed, several red-bellieds, countless downys, and heard the cackle of a pileated.

And there were blue jays. Since the family *Corvidae*, to which the blue jays and crows belong, was hit exceptionally hard by the West Nile virus this summer, it was good to see the flashy guardians of the woods doing so well. Red-tailed hawks and great horned owls also suffered from the alien virus. Hundreds were found dead or dying throughout the state. Before I returned home I saw two redtails and one great horned owl.

The cold weather has brought the rough-legged hawks south to our farm. A pair was flying, then hovering, over the hayfield, hunting for organically-fattened voles. The roughlegs spend most of their lives in the boreal regions of northern Canada and Alaska. Welcome back, you handsome raptors.

Our wintertime Cooper's hawk, too, has returned, fierce as ever; menace of the feeder birds. Flying low and fast, I saw it catch a house sparrow in the orchard. The sparrow thought it could reach the safety of the brush pile, but it misjudged and the hawk got it. Life and death.

May your Christmas be blessed with love and family and your New Year with bounty, wholesome food, and adequate rainfall.

(2002)

Weeds

In the Book of Genesis God told Adam that, as a penalty for eating of the forbidden fruit, the ground will bring forth "thorns also and thistles." The graziers here in the Central Highlands of Ohio think several more species should be added to that cursed list of thorn-in-the-side weeds. These problem weeds that are pricking me right now are relatively new to this region, appearing only in the last several decades, but they are obviously here to stay.

I will list only two – bulbous buttercup (what locals simply call, with a sigh of resignation in their voice, "those yellow flowers"), and Kentucky-31 fescue. These species are from two diverse families, but are equally successful in invading and thriving in permanent and good pastures.

While many problem weeds can be controlled, or at least held at bay in permanent pastures with carefully managed intensive grazing and timely mowing, bulbous buttercup cannot. It manages to evade all control attempts and comes back stronger and meaner than ever. Even the farmers that have used 2,4-D weed killer on the buttercups tend to admit defeat. The buttercups appear to be dead for that year; nevertheless, the following spring they are back with ferocity. Pulling it is like pulling a wart; you have to get every bit of its many-tendriled root system or it'll spring back.

For a number of years we controlled the spread of the buttercups in our pastures with the selective application of Roundup on individual plants with a hand-squeezed spray bottle. Our bottom pasture periodically floods and weed seeds come floating in. We started out spraying several dozen plants annually but finally it got to be hundreds. I then realized that, in spite of winning a number of skirmishes, we had lost the war with king buttercup.

Buttercups are particularly prolific where horses graze. The single-stomached horse seems to stratify the seeds and where it drops its manure, the grasses are slightly suppressed, the buttercup seeds sprout, and the fertility is there to boost their growth.

The tragedy of it all is that these problem forbs are here because of the follies of agribusiness. For the first half of the twentieth century, the egg market was the small-scale farmer's primary profit-maker, and these farms produced all the grain needed for laying flocks of three to five hundred hens. A local feed mill, Gold Star of Wooster, manufactured a protein supplement called Egg Elements. The farmers fed whole-grain shelled corn and oats along with the protein supplement and oyster shells. Hens and farmers flourished.

Then in the early 1960s some farmers expanded their laying flocks beyond the scale that their farms could supply with grains, so they started buying all-mash, a complete feed mixture of ground grains, protein, and minerals. Since the flocks were indoors, and soon after in cages, the egg yolks tended to be the color of low-end margarine, which was of serious concern to the savvy homemakers and chefs of that day. They remembered real eggs. Sound science quickly came to their rescue. Yellow color was added to the all-mash and the yolks actually began to look edible again. Soon every farm that harbored those larger flocks was sprouting nice, yellow-flowered plants. The feed companies were putting the flowers, and seeds, of bulbous buttercups in their layer mashes to add color to the yolks! The local commercial egg market was mostly gone by 1965, but we have a cursed reminder of those glory days.

Compared to the bulbous buttercup, Kentucky-31 fescue seems almost benevolent. When we started farming in the late 1960s, we reseeded a two-and-a-half-acre piece that had been pig pasture for too long and was populated by mostly burdock, elderberry, and bull thistle. The local soil and water conservation district gave us advice on managing the two open waterways flowing through the paddock. I had disked and seeded the field to bluegrass and white and red clover. The technician suggested I seed the waterways with K-31 fescue. Murray insisted that it would hold the soil in place and then, removing his pipe for emphasis, he looked me in the eye, "And David, it will not spread." The misstatement of the decade.

The newly seeded pasture was divided into three paddocks grazed by six to eight brood sows. This was not enough to effectively graze it, and the fescue thrived. Then I discovered (by accident, not design) a way to suppress K-31 that allows more desirable grasses and legumes to gain a foothold in the heavy sod. All winter and into May we allowed a group of yearling heifers access to the pig pasture, and they cropped the fescue as fast as it emerged. Bluegrass began to appear, I top-seeded ryegrasses and clovers and it evolved into a beautiful pasture. The fescue never recovered. It merely moved to the roadsides and ditches.

Meanwhile, here in late spring I'm seeing a few patches of yellow flowers in the nice pasture ... sigh.

Spring

Willa Cather writes in *My Antonia*, "Winter ... hangs on until it is stale and shabby, old and sullen." That must have been a winter like this one – one that forgot to leave. Here in early March there are no signs yet of an emerging spring. There has been no maple sap run, no skunk cabbage, no thaw, no migrating waterfowl, and with a foot of frozen soil, there will be no plowing for a while. On sunny, albeit cold days, the song sparrow's song does have a hint of spring in it.

Maybe the tenacious and gloomy winter is an indicator of the times we live in – milk prices are at twenty-year lows, heifer prices are on par with the milk prices, the stock market is limping like a cow with foot rot, mutual funds are off the deep end of the dock, Alan Greenspan sounds pessimistic, and war seems almost certain.

With farm product prices low, farmers are looking seriously at alternative markets. Locally, a group of twenty farmers and market-knowledgeable people have organized to study the potential for niche marketing. It will be a long tough pull to compete against the Tysons and Philip Morrises (Philip Morris and Kraft Foods are now Altria, a global-reach company that includes such household names as Marlboro, Post, Nabisco, Ritz, and Altoids), but you have to start somewhere.

For dairy there is an alternative already and that is organic. From 1998 to 2000 organic dairy products sales increased by ninety-eight percent and for the first time in 2000, more organic food was sold in conventional supermarkets than in health food stores. With the flawed and outdated science the biotech industry is using, there is a Three Mile Island just waiting to happen in the food industry. Then organic sales will go through the ceiling.

Our milk is sold through Organic Valley from Wisconsin and we are pleased with the company. Started in the mid-1980s by seven dairy farmers, Organic Valley is still very much farmer oriented and they pay fair prices. Right now it is $18.20 CWT., base price.

Organic farming is not for everyone. I know there are many skeptics in the farming communities because almost everyone remembers an organic farmer from thirty years ago that struggled and grew more weeds than corn. That farmer had likely listened to a snake oil peddler who promised his product would eliminate the need for lime, calcium, phosphorus, and other vital elements the soils may require. And thirty years ago most small farms didn't have the livestock numbers to supply the fertility their fields needed. Slowly, those farms became depleted of plant nutrients, yields decreased, and weeds, especially Canada thistles, flourished. Neighbors that helped thresh at those thistle farms loathed anything organic.

I argue that it is different today with thirty to forty dairy cows and young stock on eighty acres, where buying additional fertilizer becomes ridiculous. I know conventional farmers that haven't purchased fertilizer for ten years and grow excellent crops. All we do is apply high-calcium lime at the rate of two tons per acre every four years, which figures out at about four dollars an acre annually. The rest is livestock manure.

But, you say, I can't afford that three years' transition time to become certified organic. Remember, if you didn't use any chemicals since last spring, you already have one year toward your goal. It's the last year that may be a problem. It was for us. Because of the drought we had to buy organic hay, and sold milk on the conventional market. But it was only for a short while.

Growing corn organically is a whole lot easier than conventionally—no spray to buy, no sprayer to maintain, no fertilizer, no washing the hoppers of the planter. Imagine the simplicity and convenience. To do it, you plant later; work with the season, not the calendar. When you wait until the soil has warmed and the white oak leaves are like a squirrel's back feet, *not* ears, the corn will be up and growing within a week and you can cultivate before the weeds are on their feet. The new cultivators such as the I&J, with its S-tines and sweeps, make organic corn growing as easy as eating cherry pie. As Henry Thoreau said, "Simplify, simplify."

It is a good reminder for us to live simply so others may simply live.

(2003)

Morels

Along about the first of May, when the trilliums, spring beauties and wild geraniums are blooming, when the Canada geese are nesting, and the bobolinks and the Baltimore oriole have just returned, one's thoughts turn to mushrooms. Ah, those delectable fungi that, rolled in flour and fried in butter, melt on your tongue and leave you yearning for more, yet are so elusive to find.

There is a certain mystique surrounding the appearance of the morel—was the winter cold enough, the spring wet enough, the nights too cool, or no thunderstorms to jar them loose? Nobody really knows for sure what the reasons are for a good year of morels, or if they fail to appear, why?

There are three varieties of morels here in the hill country of Ohio; the early long-stemmed kind that has only a small pointy top which will do, but one doesn't spend hours looking for them; the early gray or dark morel which takes bifocals to locate, and the prize of them all, the large yellow sponge morel. A mess of these fine fungi is worth sacrificing a day's plowing.

When a day or two of unseasonably warm weather with accompanying thunderstorms interrupts the spring work, veteran mushroom hunters seem to be able to smell the morels and they are off to their favorite haunts, usually by themselves. One reveals a good location only reluctantly to even a best friend, and only after solemn promises have been made to not intrude later, or else the honey spot may be lost forever. It's almost like a prenuptial agreement. Friendships have gone awry over broken morel promises.

A friend and his family once

took us along to his morel haven, several counties south of us. I promised him I would never go there on my own. I have kept my word. The morning was slow; a mushroom here and there, but no great finds. In the afternoon we tried another ridge. They went down the south slope and our two daughters and I went down the north side. Soon we found a cerulean warbler and followed as it moved downhill. I was watching the warbler when Emily shouted, "Dad, look here!" Yellow morels six inches tall were standing like sentinels in the early May woodland greenery. With our binoculars, we could see mushrooms everywhere in the grove of dead red elms. After filling our bread bags, guilt overtook us and we called our friends. There were enough for everyone. We ate like royalty for a week.

For the serious morel hunters, dead elm trees with peeling bark are the first place to check for morels. I used to think it was the dead soft-wooded American elm that produced the fungi, and then I changed my mind to the red elm. Now, I closely examine every elm, and about one out of ten trees will produce mushrooms.

Not just dead elm trees are hallowed ground to the morel, it varies from season to season. Some years ash trees are good, other years sycamores and old apple orchards. I have a 130-year-old county map of all the farms that shows where the apple orchards are located. A mushroomer's treasure trove.

One of my best springs was in an open pasture that had been home to an apple orchard a hundred years before. Unfortunately, the field was too open and I soon had help gleaning the mushrooms. I did pick several nice messes before the competition made me move on.

If morels were as common as mayapples, the mystery surrounding their fickle appearance would be lost. For a week in May, we take time to join the excitement of the hunt and wonder why the morel, pushing up through the rich leafy humus of the woodlands, is always clean.

Summer

This time of the year, when the sun reaches its apex and turns back, I feel a touch of sadness for the passing of the spring; for its extravagance and its delight. The first cutting of hay is finished and the corn has been cultivated at least one time. This year the corn will barely reach my knees by the Fourth of July.

Summer officially arrived on the twenty-first, the summer solstice. Solstice simply means, in Latin, "sun stands still." In our minds the earth "stands still" and it is the sun that rises and sets and travels north for the summer and south for winter. Sometimes it's hard to visualize that we're on a journey, traveling at a speed of 1,120 miles per minute (no wonder the hay dries), around a "standing still" sun, which takes 365.24 days to complete. A distance of 590 million miles. At the same time the earth is slowly spinning, taking twenty-four hours to make one rotation. One day and a night.

For a ripening of what was seeded in the spring, it takes heat. As the sun leaves its highest angle, the warmed-up earth begins to release its heat and we call it July and August. Working in a haymow, on a torrid ninety-five-degree day with ninety percent humidity can be downright oppressive, but who complains? After two summers of drought, it is a blessing to have second-cutting hay to store in hot mows. After a cool, wet spring, the corn also needs the heat and its accompanying warm nights, as do the tomatoes, melons, peppers, and the wild raspberries and blackberries.

Too often we think that we are the center of the universe and fail to realize that India and China are home to over a third of the world's population. Food production to them is vital. Many of their people do not have the choice to travel past dozens of grocery stores until they find one that has lower prices. At our house we have the choice, but we won't, which brings to mind the old motto – THINK GLOBALLY, EAT LOCALLY.

Cheaper isn't necessarily better health-wise and socially. Our daughter bought some El Cheapo yogurt as a starter to make her own and it didn't work. There was no life in it. What do they use to make it? Styrofoam? As Art Bolduc writes in "Is the Earthworm Obsolete?": "Our only true health insurance is a sensible diet of food grown on fertile soil."

We produce most of our food on the farm, but what we don't we buy at small local food stores. We seldom get to a supermarket, but in the event we do, we patronize the locally-owned markets instead of national chains. I refuse to let our grocery money be zapped to Arkansas the evening it's spent. At least four days a week during the summer and early fall vegetable-growing season, the Buehler's (a family-owned grocery chain of around a dozen stores in Northeast Ohio) tractor-trailer passes our farm going to and from the local produce auction. They support the small-scale farmers and we should reciprocate by buying from them.

There is a love-in-action story concerning a member of the Buehler family. They own a small farm east of Wooster that still has an outside water trough. They keep fresh water in the old cement trough so the people coming into town from a distance with horse and buggy to buy groceries at Aldi's (the German-owned cheap-food chain) can water and rest their horses.

Studies have shown that a dollar spent locally may exchange hands seventeen times before leaving the community. And buying locally involves much more than food – there are hardware and houseware stores, shoe stores and feed mills, farm machinery dealers and repair shops. They need our support to succeed and we need them as suppliers in order to have a thriving agricultural community.

(2003)

Fall

What a difference a year makes. Last year, at the time of the autumnal equinox, we were still longingly scanning the western sky for rain-promising clouds. The pastures were sparse, the corn crop pitiful, and the haymows half-filled. Right now we're entering the autumn of an almost perfect growing season. The rains were timely and the temperatures pleasant (no days of over ninety degrees). Pastures have been growing profusely since April, the barns are filled with hay, and the corn crop looks promising way beyond what we hoped for when it was planted. Three times more than last year? Possibly.

To add to all of this, milk prices are improving. According to Pete Hardin in *The Milkweed* there will be serious milk supply shortages in parts of the United States before Thanksgiving. These shortages, especially in the Northeast and Southeast, could well continue through 2004. We farmers know what that means – higher on-farm milk prices and soaring prices for replacement heifers as the megadairies scramble to increase herd size.

We are being told (for two years now) that the overall economy appears to have turned the corner, but much remains iffy. Oil prices are high; Iraq, instead of funding its own reconstruction with oil revenues, is importing oil, while other important oil-producing nations are experiencing political unrest. Regardless of what we are told, our economy slides along on an oil slick and if oil and natural gas prices are high, it hits sand. I make my economic predictions by observing Alan Greenspan's brow, when he's not in hiding – it remains deeply furrowed.

Wendell Berry writes in his new book, *Citizenship Papers*: "The time will soon come when we will not be able to remember the horrors of September 11 without remembering also the unquestioning technological and economic optimism that ended on that day."

Perhaps it is time to seriously look at sun-powered farming. Grass-based farming is a step in the right direction as is anything that will help wean us from using fossil-based fuels and lessen our involvement in the turmoil of Middle-Eastern politics. Some prominent geologists are predicting that world oil production will peak in this decade and then begin to decline as consumption continues to rise. That will be the beginning of a real roller coaster ride in oil prices as demand outpaces production – and wars for the control of the oil.

We wish for all a bountiful harvest table surrounded by friends and family.

(2003)

Goose Music

Today the early hunting season for geese opened. It is the Division of Wildlife's desire to reduce the number of resident Canada geese before the migratory geese move south later in the fall. I heard neither shots nor geese.

The prolific growth of the resident goose population over the past two decades has had its downside, especially on well-manicured lawns and golf courses, where their green and white droppings aren't appreciated. The golf carts spin out. Here on our farm, I like that fertilizer. Actually, I think we have developed a neat system. Every October and November morning, starting as soon as the corn is harvested, a flock of several hundred geese will fly to the neighboring fields, feed on the waste corn, then return to our pasture field where they rest and leave their nitrogen-rich droppings. It's a simple airborne transfer of fertility from the neighbors' fields to ours. I realize that hunting is necessary to control the population, but it nevertheless saddens me to see the geese, which are family oriented, broken up so abruptly.

It was only in the latter part of the twentieth century that the Canada geese became permanent residents in Ohio. It used to be that the calls of high-flying geese were those of migrants—birds leaving their Canadian nesting grounds and flying south to warmer waters and feeding grounds for the winter. I recall a day in my boyhood when, as we were picking corn in late October, skein after skein of geese passed over and Dad said, "Bad weather is surely coming." The next day, an early season snowstorm stopped the corn harvest for about a week. The geese knew.

For the past few years, the local population of geese has not increased, or perhaps has even decreased a bit. There were no successful nests around our pond this year and some nesting attempts along the creek were flooded out by the numerous water rises from all the rainfall. Right now, a flock of around forty rest and feed on the farm. Beginning around Thanksgiving Day, our local birds will be joined by migrants out of Canada. These northern geese stay and feed in the fields until colder weather forces them further south. Last night, with the moon nearly full, the geese were flying and calling. Maybe they sensed the opening of gun season this morning and moved to larger bodies of water.

At one time, Canada geese were divided into ten distinct races or subspecies, with the cackling goose as the smallest at three to four pounds and the giant Canada goose as the largest—according to early naturalists, at twenty pounds. In recent years, these ten races have been reduced to four, with the larger races lumped into the common Canada goose. That is what we have around here, although many of the geese stocked by the departments of natural resources of many Midwestern states, beginning in the 1960s, were of the race called giant Canada goose, *Branta canadensis maxima*.

The giant Canada goose was originally at home in the Midwest and did not migrate a great distance south for the winter. Biologists declared the giant race extinct in the early 1900s. But then in 1962, giant Canada geese were discovered in a city lake in Rochester, Minnesota. Soon after, a remnant population was found nesting in cliffs along the Missouri River between St. Charles and Jefferson, Missouri. It was from these flocks that the Midwestern states restocked, and after several decades of slow but steady growth, the Canada goose is again firmly established throughout its former range. They nest in every county in Ohio.

The Canada goose, along with the white-tail deer and wild turkey, has adapted and thrived remarkably well in proximity with humans. In urban areas, they are considered only semi-wild, just like the deer. On some college campuses and golf courses, trained dogs are used to keep the geese dispersed so that their fertilizer isn't mistaken for golf balls.

It was only once that the geese caused problems for us and that was in 2001, a drought year. After the oats were harvested and the new hay began emerging, the young geese were beginning to fly, as were their parents following their annual molt and six weeks of no flying. At first, a flock of thirty came in the evenings to feed on the new growth of meadow. Then one hundred came, and then four hundred. Twice a day. They grazed the new seeding as fast as it grew and we desperately needed that twelve-acre field for fall pasture for the cows. So we let three hunters hunt for three evenings, and they shot their limit every night, which I think was three geese per hunter. The large flock dispersed into smaller groups and to other pastures and we ate our first goose meat—marinated roasted breast of goose. It tasted like fine grass-fed beef.

Overall, the geese cause no problems and bring us much pleasure. A flock doesn't pass overhead that I don't pause to watch them fly and listen to their resonant honking. And I think, what if, as Aldo Leopold wrote, "there were no more goose music?"

Winter

The early snowstorm that buried the Northeast left us with six inches. I like snow, but this year I'm not ready—we still have corn to harvest. Not much, about two dozen storm-shattered rows; just enough to keep me from enjoying the snow. So I decided to pick corn in the snow. It actually went fairly well when all was considered; snow flying, yellow ears bouncing on the wagon. What surprised me was the number of rabbit tracks in the tangle of corn. The three dogs were trying their best to chase down the cottontails. The rabbits had the advantage and easily escaped the dogs. After two rounds I gave up and so did the dogs.

All summer and fall I noticed an unusually high population of cottontails. While I was moving fence in the dark of early morning it was not unusual to see four or five in the open fields. That was rare prior to last year's West Nile virus outbreak that killed, besides horses, most of the local great horned owls, Carolina chickadees, and tufted titmice. Since the great horned owl is the cottontail's number one predator, the rabbits had few enemies and little fear. Even the careless ones lived to reproduce. And they did. If, and when, we get the corn harvested, the cottontails will move to the brushpile in the orchard and their good year ends. Last week before the snowstorm hit I heard the booming voice of a great horned owl and the call note of a chickadee. Both are likely northern birds that migrated here for the winter.

Like the cottontails', our good year ends too. Following two years of drought, this was an incredible growing season. We rotationally grazed from early April until the last week in November.

In December, whenever the weather permitted, the cows gleaned larger paddocks.

The year has been so gracious that we have our own honey again. In 2002 we lost our bees to American Foulbrood, our first experience in thirty years of beekeeping with this most-dreaded of bee diseases. (There are a number of theories why AFB is on the rise, and high on the list is Bt corn, but that is another story.) Anyway, everything had to be burned; bees and equipment.

In May (remember: a swarm in May is worth a load of hay) we got a prime swarm on our daughter and son-in-law's farm. There is a wild colony in the hollow base of a hickory tree along their field and Nate saw them swarm while he was working in the field. They let us know and Ann and I rushed over with a hive box and found the swarm clumped on the ground—another first for me—a pile of bees two and a half feet across and three inches thick. We set the hive down at the edge of the swarm and all of us, grandchildren included, knelt around the circle, faces only inches from the bees, and watched them march into their new home. I pointed out the queen as the workers escorted her inside. That was the easiest swarm I ever hived. In October we extracted three gallons of honey (leaving plenty for the bees) and got enough wax to make some honey-scented candles for Christmas.

While hiving the swarm of bees was about as *gemütlich* as things get in country living, it is not always so in rural America. Unfortunately, an economic system is never neutral, but it is a fundamental form of community that profoundly shapes society.

Emily Post wrote in 1922 that "Best society is not a fellowship of the wealthy, nor does it seek to exclude those who are not of exalted birth; but is an association of gentle-folk, of which good form in speech, charm of manner, knowledge of the social amenities, and instinctive consideration for the feelings of others, are the credentials by which society the world over recognizes its chosen members." Let that be our goal.

(2003)

Spring Peepers

I never tire of the lovesick cries of the spring peepers. Every spring, I strain to hear those first sharp calls echo from the wetlands. Some years, it is in mid-March when the little frogs begin their vernal chorus and some years not until April. When they do start calling, there is no mistaking their cries from anything else. The amphibian choir is more reliable, and a whole lot more pleasing than the *Oh-kee-leee* of the spring's first dozen red-winged blackbirds as an indicator that winter is losing out. There is simply nothing else that compares with the peepers' shrill calls as a promise of warmth to come. The earth is tilting toward the sun, the water's warming, and the peepers gustily proclaim it for all to hear.

Male peepers are the first to feel the surge of spring. They emerge and head for a wetland, likely to be the place where they were tadpoles. Once in the water, the male begins calling by inflating a balloon-like throat sac about the size of a pea and then releasing a single clear note. He repeats his sharp call every second.

Soon, those first daring peepers are joined by a multitude of their kin and the wetlands resound with their combined voices, which from a distance sound like the chiming of sleigh bells. Finding a proper simile for the triumphant calls of the peepers is difficult. To some listeners it sounds like a chirp, to some it is a yelp, and to others he peeps, hence the tiny frog's name. To me it is a beautiful call of hope.

Spring peepers require a wetland that has plants in it, or at least around the edges, because once the female arrives (attracted and guided by the male's enticing calls) and they mate, she will need submerged vegetation onto which to attach her one thousand eggs. The finest peeper place I know is a natural quarter-acre bog—what geologists would call a glacial melt–that has an abundance of buttonbushes and low willows growing in it. Around its one side are perhaps a half dozen towering pin oaks. On good, fifty-degree, early spring evenings, the little bog literally screams with musical pandemonium. Peepers call from the buttonbushes and willows and from the lower drooping branches of the oaks. The place simply reverberates with enthusiasm.

Sometime in the past decade, taxonomists switched genus on the little vernal chorister. They did keep him in the same family (*Hylidae*), but now instead of *Hyla crucifer* (tree frog) the spring peeper is called *Pseudacris crucifer* (chorus frog). Barely an inch long, the male spring peeper is often a shade smaller than his mate. What he lacks in size is made up in the volume of his call.

Unlike some other early mating frogs, such as the wood frogs, which sing for only a short time, the peepers scream from late March into May. Oftentimes, the peepers get frosted into silence, but that doesn't deter their zest for spring. As soon as the weather moderates, they are back to calling at the top of their lungs and we listen as their cheerful songs fill the spring night.

Even though spring peepers are frogs, and we tend to think of frogs as water creatures, they spend only the early spring months in water. Once the mating time is completed, the peepers head back to woodlands, where they spend the summer and autumn in and around rotting logs, beneath leaf litter, or in the dampness of woodland springs. And they remain silent. Occasionally, single males may call in the fall, but most of them won't peep again until the following March or April.

There has been a decline in the peeper numbers on our farm the last years. As the Canada goose population exploded, it was at the expense of the little frogs and their newly hatched tadpoles. The balance of nature has been upset and we need a larger predator than the red fox. A nesting goose and her mate will defend their nest from a fox; but a coyote will do just fine to occasionally dine on goose. If not goose, at least on her eggs or goslings. A few song dogs roaming up and down the creek during the nesting season, ruffling feathers of incubating geese and mallards, would help the peepers to recover.

Likewise, as the wild turkeys return to our woodlands and scratch in the leaf litter like a flock of berserk barnyard chickens, they often expose the peepers in their summer haunts. A peeper is a nice bite for a turkey. Here, too, the coyote can help in controlling the rapidly increasing turkey population.

The spring peeper's shrill call is a secure declaration that winter is ending and that there is great change taking place as March turns into April. May his tribe increase.

Spring

Although we are in the season of winter mud, spring is pushing at the barriers. Our two-year-old granddaughter breathlessly told me the robins are back in their yard. It seems the robins know when the frost is out of the ground. The morning of the robin's return I saw the first earthworm castings in the yard; a sure sign that the ground is now open and able to supply high-protein food for the birds. The maple sap is running and a few impatient plowmen have been turning furrows, even though the ground is covered with snow this morning. Typical March weather—a tease of spring followed by an onion snow. But as the old agrarian sage used to say, "Plowing down a warm March snow is as good as manure."

Whether with the robin in the dooryard, our domestic animals, the dog by the woodstove or the one herding sheep, even with the earthworms, we humans have shared a symbiotic relationship with animals for millennia. The question we need to ask ourselves is: Are we good shepherds to these animals entrusted to our care?

Recently I received a copy of a lecture given by Dr. Bernard E. Rollin at the 2004 North American Veterinary Conference in Orlando, Florida. He is a noted veterinary ethicist at Colorado State University in Fort Collins. Dr. Rollins covers the age-old human contract with our animal charges very well:

> Whether or not religion plays a significant role in your life, no educated person can deny that the Bible serves as a template for many of the concepts that undergird Western civilization. And human relationships with animals are no exceptions ... We are under a positive obligation to care for domestic animals—to place them into optimal environments that suit their biological needs and natures, protect them from predation, provide medical

attention and help in birthing, and shelter them. In turn, they provide us with their toil, their products such as milk and wool, and sometimes their lives. But while they live, they should live well.

The only way we can repay the animals in our care is with kindness, or what has been traditionally called animal husbandry. The words husband/husbandry stem from the Old Norse phrase "hus/bond," bonded to the household. It means to nurture, protect, and shelter everything within the boundaries of our household. On a diversified livestock farm that can be an extensive household.

My dad always considered it his duty, especially in the wintertime, to provide for the animals in his care – good feed, fresh water, and a clean and dry place to sleep – before returning to the house for his own meal. He always thought, or at least I got that impression, that how we treated the animals is how he expected to be treated by God. A simple practice of the Golden Rule: Treat the lives in our care with respect, love, and compassion.

Dr. Rollin goes on to say that it was a sad day when the university Departments of Animal Husbandry changed their names to Animal Science, "In less than half a century, industry had thoroughly supplanted husbandry, capital had supplanted labor, and the Biblical message was rendered irrelevant."

The sun just broke through the clouds, the snow is melting, and the Carolina wren burst out in celebratory song. The promise of renewal.

May the spring rains be timely and gentle as they water the flowers and fields.

(2004)

The Carolina Wren

For several years a pair of Carolina wrens has made our farmstead their home. Hardly a day passed in that time that one or the other didn't sing its rollicking and clear *teakettle, teakettle, teakettle* song. The wrens sing in all kinds of weather: in snowstorms, during periods of rains, and of course in sunny weather. They are such optimists that they sing every month of the year and from many different locations—from the trees and shrubs, inside the barn, on top of the pump handle, and right now from the farm shop where the pair is feeding its second brood.

The shop brood is their second one. The male finished feeding the first brood in the horse and calf barn while the female laid a second clutch and began incubating in the shop. There were five in the first clutch. We know the exact number because the young wrens, thinking they were ducks, on their maiden flight ended up in the stock watering trough. Kevin, our son-in-law, fished out five drowned young wrens. Although the wrens' bulky nest was between the ceiling joists right above the one watering trough, the young for some reason ended up in the second trough twenty feet away.

In the meantime the female had decided to reuse their last year's nest in an unzipped bicycle handlebar bag hanging in the old shop. Quite trusting of humans, the wrens continue feeding the young while I'm working in the shop. Today I was replacing knife sections of the sickle bar mower, when what I think was the male, would snap into the shop and give me a good scolding, *tieurrrrr, tieurrrr*, while holding a worm in his bill. Once satisfied that he had sufficiently put me in my place, he approached the bike bag and dropped the worm into a gaping mouth.

Carolina wrens, once considered a more southern species, move their range northward during periods of milder winters. The first edition of the *National Geographic Field Guide to the Birds of North America*, which was published in 1983, showed the northern edge of the wren's range to run on a line from south of Chicago east through northern Indiana along the south shore of Lake Erie and following the New York/Pennsylvania state lines to the coast. The third edition of the field guide, in 1999, has the wren firmly settled in southern Michigan and Ontario and halfway up in New York State.

Should a period of harsh winters occur, the spunky little songsters will be knocked southward again. That happened during the two bitter winters of 1977–1978. A pair of Carolina wrens survived the first winter in the comfort of a neighbor's heated shop. When the blizzard of January 1978 hit and Ohio experienced its lowest barometric pressure on record, with a resulting three-day blast of wind and snow, the wrens must have been caught outside and perished.

For a number of years afterward, I didn't hear their cheerful song. Then one spring, they were back in our woods as upbeat as ever. From there it was only a short flight to our shop and comfort.

I always worry a little that the barn cats will get the wrens. But if there ever was a bird that is cat savvy it's the Carolina wren.

They know and understand exactly the abilities and limits of the cats. While the male was feeding his first brood in the horse barn, Smokey's Sister, the resident cat in that building and controller of the mice and rats and my favorite, would eye the wren from five feet away and not even attempt to catch him. She knew it was futile. All the while the wren was scolding, and if I could have understood wren language I'm sure it wouldn't have been suitable for polite company.

While the Carolina wrens' nest is often cleverly placed, the nest itself isn't a neat undertaking. The one in the horse barn measured about eight inches across and was made of dried grasses, straw, dead leaves, and moss. The nest cup was delicately made. It was lined with fine grasses and horsetail hairs and had a few white feathers to cradle the five eggs. A work of art.

As long as the winters remain mild, Carolina wrens will entertain us with their songs and antics, and we cherish them.

Summer

There is an old rural proverb that "when a farmer plants in the wet he will reap in tears." I sure hope that doesn't hold true this year. It has been a tough spring to get the crops planted because of rain. After consecutive drought years in 2001 and 2002, I hear no complaints about all the rain. It's fine for us graziers, except for one hitch—a week of unseasonably warm weather in early May sent spring forward like Smarty Jones leaving the starting gate. In one week we went from mid-spring to summer and the grasses went to seed.

The rains delayed hay cutting which is to the advantage of our grassland birds. The bobolinks are feeding young. We see a pair of bobwhite quail daily at edge of the "bobolink" hayfield, and yesterday I watched a fledgling savannah sparrow make its maiden flight. In the pasture field, two young red-tailed hawks, fattened on cottontails, observe me with imperial hauteur from the edge of their nest in the walnut tree as I walk by. Around the house, the Carolina wrens are busy feeding a second brood. And with milk prices at adequate levels, things in our part of the world are pretty good. Farmers here are a happy bunch right now.

As far as the state of the rest of the world, the anxiety index remains high, especially with high fuel prices casting a shadow over the economic recovery. Analysts claim that the "terror fear factor" is adding at least five dollars to the per-barrel price of crude oil, but what they fail to say is that world demand for oil is increasing faster than they had anticipated. According to a new book by Paul Roberts, *The End of Oil*, a year ago forecasters predicted world oil demand would increase 1.3 percent in 2004. Now they say that could rise by 2.8 percent this year—or nearly three million barrels a day. The only country able to increase production by any significant amount is Saudi Arabia, which they are planning to do. Most of the other oil-producing nations are already producing at maximum volume. There is also unease in the oil industry about really how much oil is left that can be profitably extracted. Last winter, Royal Dutch Shell's CEO resigned when it became apparent that the company's oil reserves had been overstated by billions of barrels.

One reason behind this dramatic world demand for oil is China. It is now second to the United States in oil consumption. All the finished products we are importing from China (ten percent of Wal-Mart's stock) take oil to manufacture. The boom in China's economy is bringing with it a desire by the Chinese for cars, which in turn is attracting the western automobile industry like yellow jackets to a picnic. And the pressure on oil prices increases.

I find it interesting, the almost child-like trust and faith that God will provide a way for us to continue unimpeded in our gluttonous ways. Surely alternatives will be forthcoming. There is one already, they say—hydrogen. A neighbor was so enthusiastic over the glowing prospect of hydrogen that he almost invested in Sure-Power systems, a hydrogen fuel cell company, back in the late 1990s when its stock was $140 a share. How practical is near-term use of hydrogen to power our massive fossil fuel-driven economy? Another new book, this one by Joseph J. Romm, *The Hype About Hydrogen*, provides an answer to that question. Say for example, the new "FreedomCar" hits the road and we need refueling stations for compressed hydrogen. Fifteen tanker trucks will be needed to serve the same number of vehicles as one gasoline tanker does today. If the hydrogen needs to be trucked three hundred miles, they will use forty percent of all the energy they deliver just to transport it. Paul Roberts quotes a hydrogen engineer, "I'm afraid that when we finally get people to stop associating hydrogen with bombs and the Hindenburg explosion, the next word they'll think of will be 'scam'." Sure-Power stock is down to six dollars.

Likewise, wind and solar-powered energy also have shortcomings—becalmed and overcast days when no power is generated. Only time will tell how things will turn out, but one thing we do know and that is: "the times, they are a-changing."

When you are at the library getting *The End of Oil*, pick up a copy of *Brave New World*, Aldous Huxley's 1932 classic satire. *That* may provide the best insight for our current times.

(2004)

Fall

We are approaching the end of another extraordinary growing season, albeit a bit on the wet side. The wet spring was followed by a wet summer with many cool and pleasant days. August looked as green and lush as May. The tomatoes were late in ripening and the same heat units needed to ripen the tomatoes are needed to mature the corn. In case of an early killing frost like last year, some corn is going to be hurt, especially the replanted corn. We have only an acre of that late corn and plan on ensiling it along with more mature corn.

Our last first cutting of hay was made in early summer, which delayed the succeeding cuttings. Right now we are getting ready to cut the third crop. We need around five hundred small bales yet to see us to April and new grass. All eyes are on Hurricane Ivan, a massive category five storm, and whether he will churn up through the Gulf States and affect our haycutting here.

Are these powerful hurricanes a result of the earth heating up, which in turn spurs more violent storms?

This summer some unusual behavior occurred in a number of large nesting colonies of wild birds that may be a result of climate change. In North Dakota thousands of white pelicans abandoned their nesting grounds, leaving eggs and chicks behind. Michael McCarthy, who is an Environment Editor, also wrote that tens of thousands of seabirds in Scotland's Northern Isles had nesting failure. Ornithologists said it is the year without young. Eggs have not been laid; where eggs have been laid, they have not hatched; where they have hatched, the chicks have died in the nest, and the tiny numbers of chicks that have left the nest have not lasted long.

There has been seabird nesting failure in the Northern Isles before, McCarthy wrote, but the extent of this year's catastrophe is entirely unprecedented. At a cliff near Sumburgh Head on

Shetland's southern tip, where 1,200 pairs of guillemots assembled to breed in the spring, not a single chick has been produced. Arctic terns, of which the last census in 2000 recorded 24,716 breeding pairs in Shetland, have produced no chicks at all in the south part of the islands, according to Peter Ellis, the local representative of the Royal Society for the Protection of Birds.

The reason is starvation, and the reason for the starvation is thought to be climate change. The once-teeming stocks of sand eels, the small fish on which nearly all the local seabirds depend, have vanished, leaving the parent birds unable to feed their young—or even themselves. Scientists believe the steadily rising temperature of the water in the North Sea, which has gone up by two degrees centigrade in twenty years, is having a calamitous effect on the sand eels, essentially a cold-water species. After several years of decline, they have vanished almost completely in the waters around the Northern Isles.

Martin Heubeck of Aberdeen University, who has recorded seabird breeding at Sumburgh Head for almost thirty years, said: "This has been an almost unbelievably bad breeding season. The scale of the breeding failure of the guillemots is unprecedented in Europe." The fact that guillemots are suffering shows the extent of the fish famine. Arctic terns and kittiwakes can only catch sand eels near the sea's surface, but guillemots can fly many miles in search of sand eel shoals and then dive to depths of more than three-hundred feet to catch them. But now they are returning with empty beaks and stomachs.

Here at our farm, the two-hundred pairs of cliff swallows left early. Usually about two-thirds of the birds in the colony raise a second brood. This year none did. At first I attributed their early departure to kestrel harassment, but after talking to a neighbor who has a much larger colony (over five hundred pairs), he reported the same phenomenon. He even thinks his birds abandoned young in the nest. Why? We don't know.

On the other hand, the pair of Carolina wrens in the yard produced a bumper crop of young (two or three broods). Buoyant birdsong should abound through the next year.

Summer can be a slow time when everyone is busy nurturing land and family.

(2004)

White Snakeroot

Today the autumnal equinox occurs; that time when daylight and darkness are almost equal and the noon sun hangs straight above the equator. Summer ends and the season of fall begins. Why fall? Was it shortened from "fall of the leaf" as the season was called in 1500s England?

Even though autumn now officially begins, the signs of change were evident for several weeks already. The angle of light is different, giving the trees a golden hue even though few leaves have actually changed color. Here and there a few maples are beginning to show some reds and yellow, and the linden is slowly turning from green to yellow. And of course, the black gum has some leaves of crimson. The gum can't wait for autumn to display its colors.

Likewise, in the insect world there is a winding down; that preparation for the end of summer. Last evening, with the temperature at seventy degrees, I biked along a woods where in August's heat dozens of katydids called out their names. Now, instead of a multitude rasping, I heard only two. And their songs were a halfhearted *katy-de* instead of the robust *katy-didn't* of a month ago. Surprisingly, I saw several late fireflies blinking their lights over a hayfield. Even their light seemed weak and unsure.

The tall fall flowers, however, are thriving. Night before last our daughter brought home a bouquet of assorted wildflowers. She had tall and flat-topped goldenrods, a deep purple tall ironweed, a late and lovely lavender joe-pye weed, and wild sunflowers.

To add white to the yellows and purple of the bouquet, she brought white snakeroot, with its sprays of cottony-white flowers.

White snakeroot is an interesting plant, and a deadly one. It is a plant that brought much grief to pioneer families. Nine-year-old Abraham Lincoln's mother, Nancy Hanks Lincoln, died from snakeroot poisoning. Since the two- to three-feet tall snakeroot grows along woods' edges and in clearings, it was grazed in late summer and autumn by the settlers' cows. The poison in snakeroot, tremetol, is fat-soluble, so it is concentrated in milk and was passed on to the families that drank the milk. The poisoned milk caused a disease called "milksick." In animals the disease was called "trembles."

During the nineteenth century, the dreaded disease would periodically appear and the frontier doctors had no cure or idea what caused it. Twenty-five percent of its victims died within ten days of the onset of the first symptoms of milksick, which were severe abdominal cramps and vomiting, followed by muscle fatigue. In a few days, they entered a coma that often led to death.

Although the physicians were puzzled by the mysterious disease, farmers noticed that milksick most often occurred in late summer and early autumn in dry years. They suspected their animals were eating plants they wouldn't touch in normal rainfall years.

In 1841, John Rowe, an Ohio farmer, brewed a batch of snakeroot leaves and fed the extract to a pig, which died twelve hours later. Rowe then offered snakeroot to a steer and a calf that refused to eat the plants until all their other feed was withheld for several days. Finally the animals ate the snakeroot, developed trembles, and died. Rowe announced his discovery in a local paper, but because he hadn't kept detailed notes of his research, the medical profession, unfortunately for the disease's sufferers, dismissed Rowe's conclusions. As late as 1906, a death from milksick occurred in Erie County, Ohio.

It was not until 1909 that botanist and eccentric Bowling Green State College professor, Edwin L. Moseley, became interested in milksick and ran careful animal tests. He proved beyond a doubt that white snakeroot was the culprit the plant farmers had suspected for many years. By then, the disease had almost died out as more land was cleared and snakeroot retreated from the clearings. The increase in dairy herd size helped too, for the milk of the occasional daring cow that ate snakeroot was diluted with untainted milk, making it safe to drink.

In 1929, researchers finally isolated and identified snakeroot's poison. They named it *tremetol*, likely for the tremors it caused. *Tremetol* is a complex, fat-soluble alcohol.

The white snakeroot in our bouquet doesn't look deadly, but I'm not going to feed it to the pigs.

Winter

By the calendar the shortest day of the year has come and gone. The winter solstice occurred on December 21, when the year reached its nadir. That is the time when the sun stands still before slowly turning and beginning its climb into the sky toward another spring and summer. I rejoice. Even though we have passed our earliest sunset, sunrise will continue to lag into the New Year, giving us those generously long and dark mornings to relax and read following the chores and breakfast.

Winter actually begins long before the solstice. Botanists say the season starts when the average daily temperature falls below forty-three degrees Fahrenheit, the point where plant growth stops and winter dormancy begins. The naturalist Hal Borland, who lived in New England, insisted that their winter began on the first full moon after the middle of November, which would have been November 30 (the month's second full moon) this year. [*editor's note: winter of 2001*] The moon the Indians called the Cold Moon.

For a farmer, winter begins when we move the cattle from pastures to the barn, which can be anywhere from mid-November to the middle of December. Every farmer tries to graze as long as possible to save on winter feed. This year, Christmas Eve was the first time for the season that all the animals were indoors—when the cows, calves, horses, goats, dogs, and cats were all nestled down in the comfort of the barn for the long winter night. It was necessary on account of a wind-driven rain that changed to sleet. It was, as an oldtimer described, a Nor'easter: "First it rained, then it blew, then it sleet, then it snew."

While the domestic animals are snugged in for the winter, wild creatures must cope the best they can in this cold and snow. Some are well adapted to survive in this bitter weather, such as the horned larks that feed on cracked grain that I spread for them here in early winter. The hardy larks are northern birds that migrated here for the winter. They appear impervious to wind and cold. Actually, they seem to enjoy it. As I write this, a red-breasted nuthatch is busy eating sunflowers at the feeder–another little visitor from the North that isn't afraid of the cold.

Unlike migratory birds, which travel south thousands of miles to more agreeable climates, mammals tend to stay in fairly small areas and tough out the winter. (Some ungulates do travel great distances from summer to winter ranges, such as the caribou in the Arctic and Africa's wildebeests.) A few mammals hibernate during the cold and dark months. Right now the woodchuck is curled in a ball in its leaf- and grass-lined nest somewhere in the labyrinth of its underground burrow. The nest is below the frost line, so the woodchuck remains comfortable living off the body fat it gained in the fall.

Raccoons too, semi-hibernate, surviving on the energy of stored fat gained from a summer and autumn of gluttonous living on sweet corn and chicken. By February the males will be out looking for females, even if there is a foot of snow on the ground.

The opossum though, is not so fortunate. An animal better adapted to the warmer climates south of the Mason-Dixon Line, the poor animal suffers if our northern winters are severe. The opossum can be butter-fat in the fall, but by Christmas time its reserves are depleted and it has to eat.

The snowstorm earlier this week left a fine dusting of powdery snow over the upper barn floor. Among the numerous barn cat tracks crisscrossing the floor the following morning, was a set of opossum footprints. Similar to the imprint of a human hand with its protruding thumb, these tracks trailed along the edge of the haymow to the cow feed hopper, where the possum fed on spilled grain. From there, the tracks led to a stack of straw bales where it obviously has its winter den. From a summer diet of bird eggs, carrion, and pokeberries, cow feed must be pretty meager fare. I felt sorry for the hungry possum and left a handful of dog food by the feed hopper. The next morning every nugget was gone.

Yesterday when I went to bring home a load of firewood, I walked along the creek to see what was up. The only creature that was stirring near the water was the mink. The mink doesn't store fat for the winter and is as lean and tough as a marathon runner. It has to eat regularly. I followed its tracks across the ice and saw where it traveled behind overhanging banks looking for mice or possibly a cottontail. Another set of tracks that crossed the pasture field between the woods and creek were those of the red fox. Trotting in a straight line, the tracks headed south for a field that held the promise of meadow voles.

In this season of short daylight hours, many people get the winter blues. Medical science calls the condition Seasonal Affective Disorder (SAD). The symptoms include mild depression, fatigue, increased sleep, and weight gain (that desire to hibernate?). The malaise can be corrected by exposure to bright lights, walking outdoors for at least thirty minutes each day, or a trip to Tucson.

This is also the holiday season, a celebration of a holy day, a time of reverence for life and the spiritual meanings implicit to it. I think of these beautiful lines in *The Book of Common Prayer*: "O Lord, support us all through the day long, until the shadows lengthen and evening comes, and the busy world is hushed, and the fever of life is over, and our work is done. Then in Thy mercy grant us a safe lodging, and a holy rest, and peace at last."

The Barn as Haven

This morning the wind was from the northeast; a bitter, biting wind accompanied by a haze of powder-fine snow that sifted in through every crack in the upper barn doors to form in neat little drifts on the threshing floor. In spite of the piercing wind, the lower level of the 150-year-old barn was comfortable enough that we worked without our chore coats as we went about doing the morning milking and other barn chores.

The reason for our comfort on this cold morning was that our barn bank is on the east side of the barn, unusual for this part of the country. Most of the barns have their big upper doors facing west or south, to catch the summer's prevailing winds for pleasant conditions while stacking hay and threshing grains. The west banks naturally afford wind protection in the lower barn during the cold months.

When my grandfather moved our barn to its present location from a quarter mile away in 1925, he had no choice but to bank it toward the east because of the slope of the land. In any case, it has served our family well ever since as a home for livestock on the first level and their stored feeds above. The two hay holes, besides providing a place to drop hay and bedding to the lower story, serve as ventilating shafts to draw out stale air from below. It is only in extremely cold weather that we close the hay holes to prevent a draft and keep the animals warmer.

The definition of a "bank" barn is that there is an earthen driveway built up to the second story of the barn so that wagons and machinery can be driven directly into the sidewall to the top floor to unload forage and grain. In our rolling terrain, most of the banks leading to the barns are not steep. Some are almost level. I have a friend who, as a young man during the 1940s, worked on

a Wisconsin dairy farm that had an awfully steep barn bank. He claimed the most difficult thing he did on that farm was to back loads of hay up that bank with an Allis-Chalmers WC tractor. One should have had five hands he said – two to hold both hand brakes, one to shift gears, and two to steer (no power steering then.)

Our barn is of traditional Swiss/German mortise-and-tenon design with a sixty-foot forebay along the driveway side. The forebay is a self-supporting roof that gives quick shelter to humans and animals during sudden summer thunderstorms – where farmers sit on buckets or bales and talk and wait for the storm to pass. Most of the timbers are hand-hewn white oak with built-in ladders (hand-hewn rungs) leading to the haymows. While many barns are one-hundred feet or more in length, ours is eighty feet, with four twenty-foot bays. To the right of the threshing bay, or floor, are two six-hundred bushel granaries to store small grains after harvest.

Soon after the barn was moved, my grandfather and uncle had Lou Halfhill, (an extremely gifted carpenter when sober), build a 40x40-foot addition to the barn. Locally, that part of the barn is called the straw and cattle shed. It became an integral part of the barn when wheat was a vital cash crop on the small farm and a dry place was needed to store straw, instead of using an outside stack. It serves very well with a threshing machine, since the straw is blown loose into the straw shed to be pushed down and used for bedding in the winter.

It was in this pile of loose straw that our children honed their skills as sky divers. When their grandfather (he was the thresherman) wasn't watching, they would climb out over the blower of the threshing machine and leap off into the loose straw below. There they would have twenty-foot slides – down the face of the straw pile – to disappear into a swirl of straw and chaff.

But times change, and as the saying goes, we change with time. In 1960, we put in our last loose hay and thereafter started baling. The hay track and carrier and harpoons are still in place and ready for use should the need arise. For many years, we would stack bales all the way up to the hay track at the peak of the barn. As my neighbor would say, "Stacked so full that the pigeons have to walk."

For years I was the mow man. The children or my dad, sometimes a neighbor's boy, or my wife, would put the bales on the elevator and I stacked them in the mow. It was always a family affair, and still is. One difference, I have been shifted from the mow to the wagon. The mows aren't filled to the track anymore because we do more round baling, which lightens the workload. But, in my opinion, small square bales are still the most convenient and practical way to feed hay in traditional barns and a lot less forage is wasted.

Although we practice intensive grazing and our cows are out on grass from April to December, we like to grow oats for grain and straw, corn for grain, and harvest enough hay so that we don't have to buy feed in this volatile market. Part of the pleasure of growing oats, I'll admit, is the harvest time; another family affair. Also, I believe oats are an underrated grain for livestock, especially for calves and horses. And as long as the supply lasts, we mix oats and corn for the dairy herd.

Besides, I'm an oatmeal aficionado. For some reason, I get satisfaction eating from the same granary that the chickens, calves, cows, and horses do. As Samuel Johnson famously quipped, after moving from Scotland to England, "In England the horses eat oats, in Scotland the people do." The problem with eating oats is that the grains have to be dehulled. Our local miller has a dehuller and roller mill and prepares a nice rolled oats, but he still misses some hulls.

This year, we plan to sow some naked oats, so called because they thresh free of the hulls like wheat and would only need to be cleaned and rolled. Naked oats, *Avena nuda*, have been grown for centuries by farmers who appreciate their value for feeding to horses, chickens, young stock, and for their own tables. Since naked oats don't yield as much per acre and tend to lodge when grown in soils of high fertility, few farmers grow the variety anymore. My concern is whether they will have the hearty flavor of our regular oats.

Once the oats are harvested and the bales stored, the barn can be used for other purposes. Perhaps the finest ceremony for the traditional barn is a wedding. We have friends whose son and his wife were married in their barn. He lived in D.C. and she in New York City and all their friends traveled to the Midwest and sat on backless benches on a humid July evening while the bride and groom exchanged their vows. Overhead, clinging to a rough-hewn rafter, a luna moth took it all in.

Most of the old barns have well-worn flooring that has been pounded for many years by hoofs and wheels and thus don't furnish the ideal surface for religious services. To remedy the roughness, the farmer spreads his finest hay, usually a second or third cutting of legume and grass mixed hay, on the floor for a covering. To me, the aroma of that new hay beats any incense imaginable. Afterward, the "carpeting" is recycled through the animals and the barn reverts to being a keeper of the beasts.

Spring

This winter, "The winter of torment," as Gene Logsdon writes, was a season of extremes. In all my years of farming, it was the most difficult to get things done. In the fall, the corn was late and we had only a few days of decent conditions to get it harvested. Oftentimes the weather allowed only a half-day of frozen ground to get some manure out and firewood in. Once the ground did freeze, there was too much snow for much outdoor work. Then it rained, the ground thawed, the rain turned to snow before the ground refroze and the snow covered a quagmire of mud.

The most interesting event, though, and painful for many people, was the severe ice storm of late December. As a rule, most of our ice storms occur when the weather is moderating and snow turns to rain and freezes. As the day goes on, it continues to warm up, the ice melts, and the crisis passes. This time, the weather was warm and as the temperature dropped, it started to rain and then changed to freezing rain. The ice kept building on the trees until many reached their breaking points, and what I took to be lightning were actually flashes of electricity as broken trees took down wires. The ice stayed on the trees for four days and the landscape simply sparkled, particularly in the late afternoons. Parts of Ohio were without electricity for over a week.

Our worst crisis was the windpump, which supplies water for the livestock. I had set it off and everything was frozen solid into the "off" position. I climbed up forty feet on ice-covered steps with a hose of hot water to melt half an inch of ice so that it would unlock. After fifty gallons of hot water, and me looking like a Japanese snow monkey, the windpump swung into gear.

After the ice storm, our yard was a disaster. My mother loved shade trees, but unfortunately, she planted too many softwoods such as silver maples and Chinese elm. The storm was especially rough on softwoods.

We like to have a continuous brushpile (an accumulation of orchard tree trimmings, storm-downed limbs, landscaping mistakes) in the orchard for the cottontails and other wild things. Early last fall, Ann and I burned the massive pile of brush, along with some old shingles, before the rabbits moved in for the winter. The fire did evict two cottontails and one Norway rat. The vigilant dogs got the rat.

By the end of the ice storm, the cottontails had a new and even bigger home of brush and branches and they promptly moved back in.

But as the saying goes, "Every cloud has a silver lining." The other morning early, one of our ten-degree March mornings, there was a knock on the door. A young man was out riding his horse and saw our new brush pile and wondered when I planned to burn it?

I answered, "Not this winter, because the rabbits claimed the deed again."

"Yes," he said, "I counted four along the edges when I rode around it." Then he added, "Could I possibly have that pile of branches later this spring?"

I immediately thought of the three little pigs and asked, "Are you building a new home?"

No, in his spare time (he is a home builder) he makes twig lawn furniture and arbors and he would have use for most of the storm-downed wood. He saw opportunity in disaster. Amazing.

"Of course," I said, "the brushpile is yours once the mild days of spring arrive, crocuses bloom, peepers call, and the cottontails move out to the fields to rear their young."

(2005)

The Rat

Scientists claim a rat can tread water for three days before drowning. If that is the case, the rat I discovered in our half-filled water trough must have been in for at least four days, because it was dead. The rat was a victim of the smooth sides of the Rubbermaid stock tank; once in the water it couldn't claw its way back to the top as it could have in a concrete trough. Only rarely does a rat make such a blunder.

The Norway rat, (*Rattus norvegicus*) wears the label "commensal," meaning literally that they share our table. Rats are considered the most numerous and successful and destructive furry mammal on earth. There are almost no barriers they can't dig under, climb over, travel around, or swim through. Since they are generalized animals, rats will eat almost anything and live almost anywhere, as long as it is near humans.

In spite of its common name, the Norway rat is not a native of that lovely land. But since the burly burrower came to this country as a stowaway on sailing vessels, the busy maritime nation of Norway got the credit for delivering the rat to our east coast cities around 1775.

Originally at home in Asia, Norway or brown rats overran Europe in the 1700s. Up until then, the black or roof rat (*Rattus rattus*) was the common rat of Europe and was the bearer of the plague, Black Death. When a plague-infected roof rat died, its disease-carrying fleas sought a new host and that included humans. In three years during the early 1300s, the plague left twenty-five million people dead in Europe. Where Norway rats abound, roof rat populations decline. There seems to be little tolerance between the two species.

From the eastern cities, *Rattus* hitchhiked westward in the hay stored in covered wagons and by rail, and by the 1920s had settled in all the western states. The main reason for the rat's rapid conquest of the nation was its remarkable reproductive ability. A female will have her first litter of five to seven young when she is only three or four months old. Soon after the young are weaned at three weeks of age, she has another litter. Shortly after that her offspring begin reproducing and there will be rats everywhere.

Even though rats will live anywhere–in cities, any littered dark corner or sewer will do–on farms they prefer to live in underground burrows like the *Rats of NIMH*. They are especially fond of the edges of corncribs, and buildings that house livestock where there is a nearby source of food. Our chicken house seems to be preferred by every rat that comes along. Coming out at night while the hens are on the roost, the rats have the run of the coop. With ground corn and oats and water and an occasional overlooked egg, what more could a rat desire?

Rats are primarily vegetarian, with an occasional meal of meat. I once watched a house sparrow searching for waste grain in the hog house. When the bird hopped near an opening along the wall, a rat darted out, pounced on the bewildered sparrow, and quickly carried it into its burrow. Meat was on the menu.

As that sparrow found out, a rat can be a ferocious animal. If a rat finds an opening into a brooder house where there are baby chicks, it will not stop killing until every chick is dead. But as a rule, rats are shy and do their venturing under the cover of darkness. Farmers say for every rat one sees, there are twenty-five others hiding somewhere.

In physical appearance the rat isn't very attractive. Its fur tends to be coarse and is grayish-brown above and paler on its belly. The older the rat, the browner its coat. We once tore down an old corncrib that had sunk to the ground and had become a rat haven. As we neared the end of the dismantling the rats began to leave and race for cover, but Sam, our black Lab, caught every one.

Finally when we were down to the last floorboard, the matriarch dashed for the safety of the distant scrap pile. Sam caught up with her with barely a second to spare. An old female, the rat was the largest one I've ever seen. It was as brown as a muskrat and weighed almost two pounds.

In spite of being called the Devil's Lapdog, the rat as a laboratory animal has saved countless human lives. And *Rattus* has added to our lore and language: he "fights like a cornered rat," and we all know about "the rat race."

Summer

Friends keep passing on to me books and articles to read that tend toward the gloomy end of the economic spectrum. They know sports don't interest me and that I watch the world economic scene for entertainment. This morning's paper announced, on page four of the business section, that world oil prices jumped over two dollars a barrel to almost fifty-five dollars. Refiners are concerned about the availability of heating oil for next winter, the paper said. Yet the Dow went up almost a hundred points because the Dutch voted down the European Union's constitution and a Federal Reserve board executive said we're in the "eighth inning of interest rate hikes." Perhaps it is sports after all.

Peter Peterson, former chairman of the Federal Reserve Bank in New York, chairman of The Blackstone Group, and a moderate Republican, put it most succinctly in his book *Running on Empty*, "We are not paying our own way," he says. "As a nation, we are running on empty. If the ultimate test of a moral society is the heritage it leaves to its grandchildren, I would say we are failing that test."

Peterson quotes Paul Volcker, former chairman of the Federal Reserve Board, as saying we face a seventy-five percent chance of a financial crisis within five years. Robert Rubin, former economic chief under President Clinton, likewise says we are confronting "a day of serious reckoning" and that "the traditional immunity of advanced countries like America to a Third World-style crisis isn't a birthright."

Peterson continues, "The new reality is our huge foreign currency account deficits. Currently we import $4.4 billion of foreign capital a day ... our borrowing is at unprecedented levels for an industrialized power. None of the specialists believe that this is sustainable, and half of the experts say we risk a hard landing. America must consume less and save more, export more and import less."

What these men–among our best and brightest–are telling us is that we are simply going broke. But as Carl Jung, one of the fathers of psychology said, "People cannot stand too much reality." It is business as usual.

What, you may ask, has this to do with farming? A lot. Sociologists agree that the first order of business for any nation is feeding the population. And that is why it is so hard to understand why China made the enormous strategic blunder of opting for two cars in every garage. Is it an attempt of a totalitarian government to hang on to power rather than provide real leadership? Not only will they now pave over their best arable lands, but the back side of the bell curve of world oil reserves will become a slick slope as consumption increases dramatically in China. Lester Brown will have to ask again, "Who will feed China?"

Back to farming–James Howard Kuntsler writes in his book, *The Long Emergency*, "Food production is going to be an enormous problem. As industrial agriculture fails due to a scarcity of oil and gas-based inputs, we will certainly have to grow more of our food closer to where we live, and do it on a smaller scale. The American economy of the mid-twenty-first century may actually center on agriculture, not information, not high tech, not "services" like real estate sales or hawking cheeseburgers to tourists. Farming."

I have been telling farmers that they should donate their development rights to a farmland trust because it is a win-win deal. As suburbia collapses in the coming fuel crunch, their farms will be much more valuable in dollars as food producers than as building sites for McMansions and starter castles.

It has been a good spring. The cool weather slowed the progress of the season so that it could be savored like a good meal. Peepers called for two months, the bird migration doodled along, the pastures were slow, the bees are well, and now the corn is ready to be cultivated, and there are two-thousand bales of nice hay waiting for this afternoon ...

(2005)

Fall

One of the pleasures of summer is to sit on the porch swing and watch a rip-snorting thunderstorm break a drought. Lightning flashes, thunder cracks, trees bend and sway, squirrels seek the lee of the maple's trunk, the house shudders, and the dogs appreciate the shelter of the roof and my company. After weeks of watching promising storm clouds gather in the northwest only to part and drench Wooster to the north and shower Charm to the south, our turn came.

Soaked by several inches of rain along with all the free nitrogen, things are really looking green and good. The pastures are rebounding and the corn shows signs of an excellent crop. Plus, as we approach the end of summer, the heat has relented. A front moved through and instead of high sixties or seventy degrees at 5:00 A.M., this morning it was fifty-five degrees and I wore a light coat to move the fence. Local weather watchers tell me we've had somewhere between twenty and thirty days of ninety degrees or above.

Besides the cooler temperatures, I had another pleasant surprise this morning while moving the fence. In the gathering dawn that was just beginning to wash out Orion and Sirius, I saw a fairly large bird flying low across the field headed straight at me. Aha, a barn owl! When the owl was above me (twenty feet) it turned its monkey face, gave me a once-over, and flew directly for our barn. It was still too dark to follow its flight all the way, but later in the day I checked the silo and there it was. No wonder the barn pigeons have been so skittish the last while.

The barn owls are thriving in this region, with at least two dozen pairs nesting in the greater community. When West Nile virus severely reduced the great horned owl population in 2002, it opened a window of opportunity for the preyed-upon barn owl, and they have done well. A reminder: We need to put up an owl nesting box inside the barn.

This summer's drought, while not nearly as severe, did take me back to 1988, because both times we were cutting oats when the break finally came. I was at the far end of the field when the darkening northwestern sky began looking seriously ominous. This one is for real, I thought, it won't part and pass us by. A rush for the barn, a quick tarping, and a sixty-yard sprint for the porch swing to take it all in. It happened two days in a row and we didn't mind the interruptions at all. As my dad would tell me, "When it rains on the mowed hay, remember that it is also raining on the corn and pastures and gardens." Then Katrina gave us four inches and the promise of lush autumn pastures and the drought became a memory.

While we were blessed in getting rain, there are regions – Illinois and parts of the East – that weren't so fortunate and suffered lost production. For that reason we don't want to be too euphoric.

As frost returns and then pauses for Indian summer and the leaves turn crimson and golden and the woodchucks fatten on late clover, may our woodpiles be stacked with seasoned oak and the barns and cellars well-stocked with the bounty of the harvest season.

(2005)

Barn Owls

I have seen fewer than a dozen barn owls in my lifetime and heard their wild nighttime cry perhaps twice as often. Only twice have I seen them on our farm. The first time was when I was six years old; a pair of barn owls spent several days staring at us from the highest beams of our barn. The second time was when one used our silo for a daytime roosting place for one day.

So I was pleased several weeks ago when I was walking home from the neighbors' one evening and heard the call of a hunting barn owl. The owl called four or five times at regular intervals as it flew up the valley toward the Keims' and Troyers'. I had hopes for a nest of owls somewhere in a neighboring barn or silo.

Actually, the call of the flying barn owl is more like a screech or scream than a call. Gilbert White wrote in *The Natural History of Selborne*, "Whiteowls … scream horribly as they fly along." When White wrote this in the late 1700s, barn owls often nested in England's church towers, and the owls' nightly screams, heard over the nearby cemeteries, gave rise to many imaginations and superstitions. I do not find the scream of the barn owl horrible at all. I think it is a pleasant nighttime sound; a whole lot nicer than blaring boom boxes marring the quietude of summer nights.

Gilbert White called the barn owl the "white owl," and when compared to our other native owls, the barn owl does appear almost white. Its feathers are white with orange/tan ends. It is also the only owl with a white heart-shaped face. For that reason, many farmers years ago called them monkey-faced owls.

Barn owls begin nesting by late March. The eggs are laid at two-to-three-day intervals and incubation begins soon after the first egg is laid. The average clutch size is five to seven eggs, and by the time the last egg hatches, the first owlet may be two weeks old. Many times, the last chick is trod over and pushed back by

its siblings and may end up being eaten by the older ones. At seven or eight weeks of age, the young leave the nest but remain in the area and will be brought food by their parents.

Barn owls moved into the eastern United States soon after the woodlands were cleared and converted to farms. Here in Ohio, the breeding population of barn owls peaked in the 1930s and 1940s. In 1935 barn owls nested in eighty-four out of Ohio's eighty-eight counties. The nesting population of barn owls in Ohio went into a steep decline during the 1950s, and by 1970, only ten to twenty known pairs were nesting in the state.

There were a number of factors involved in the barn owls' disappearance here in Ohio. Bruce Peterjohn writes on the dramatic decline of the barn owls in *The Birds of Ohio*:

> ... changing land-use patterns were critical. Many grassy pastures and hayfields were converted to cultivated fields. Near urban areas, grasslands were turned into housing developments. Suitable nest sites were also lost when many abandoned buildings were torn down. However, other factors were probably involved, since barn owls disappeared from areas where suitable habitats were still available.

Yes, I could add, predation by great horned owls. A week after I heard the barn owl, I went to harrow a six-acre field in preparation of sowing oats. Soon after the field was plowed we had a cloudburst—three inches of rain in half an hour—so the soil was packed down fairly hard. When I started in the one end, I noticed something white in the middle of the field and as I got closer I saw the "white" was a scattering of plucked wing and breast feathers of a barn owl. On closer examination I also found several incriminating splotches of whitewash left by a great horned owl. From the evidence, it appeared the great horned owl caught its smaller cousin, carried it to the safety of the middle of the bare field, ate its fill, and then took what was left to its nest for the young great horned owls, which by this time are almost fully grown and demand a tremendous amount of food.

Locally, the barn owl is getting generous support from owl enthusiasts. Paul Boyd, a semi-retired farmer from near Berlin, Ohio, has twenty-three barn owl nesting boxes out in barns that he regularly monitors. Because of Paul's and other owl lovers' efforts, our county has the highest number of nesting barn owls in the state.

This year, at least seven of Paul's boxes have owls nesting in them, several fewer pairs than last year. Paul blames the lower numbers on last summer's drought that caused a drop in the meadow vole population, the barn owls' main fare. But the owls do adjust to other prey. Paul has checked nesting boxes that had mourning doves, a robin, and a blackbird in them. One box that housed seven young owls had four dead adult Norway rats in it for their next meal.

Once the young owls fledge, they tend to wander aimlessly over a broad region. According to banding records, there isn't a pronounced migration southward for the winter. Last year twenty-one barn owls were counted on the three local Christmas Bird Counts. Paul worries that a cold winter or an ice storm could kill many of the local over-wintering owls.

Paul's dimensions for the barn owl nest boxes are as follows: forty inches in length, sixteen inches high, and fourteen inches deep (see accompanying illustration). Half of the top is a lid and hinged for easy access. If the box can be mounted flush against the wall of the barn, a three-sided box is sufficient. If not, four sides are needed. The six-inch by six-inch entrance opening should be six inches above the floor of the nest box and at least two inches in from the end. He stressed that the box be mounted where it is relatively easy to monitor. Preferably, the entrance hole to the box should be on a side or end of the barn where there is no roof, such as an overbay, beneath it.

For years I have debated whether to put up a nesting box because I was afraid that barn owls may be detrimental to our cliff swallow colony nesting along our barn's eaves. Paul said that should be no problem. He monitors one nesting box that is right underneath a thriving cliff swallow colony. The owls become active at dusk and are ignored by the swallows.

The other morning I heard another barn owl scream. I think I will make a nesting box and get it mounted before we fill the mow with hay.

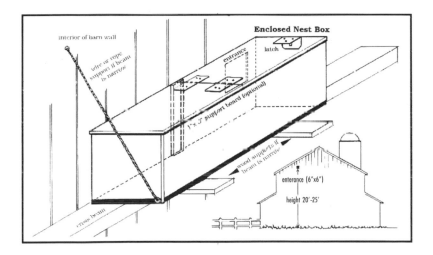

Winter

Winter came in a rush – from cutting and splitting firewood in shirtsleeves one day to rain and snow and windchill temperatures in the teens the next. The sudden cold simplified bringing in the heifers from their summer pasture. Instead of high-tailing it in ten different directions in the howling snow squall, the heifers made a beeline for their winter quarters and to the hay waiting for them. What made it seem so cold was that we weren't used to it. Following one of the warmest summers on record, we had become thin-skinned by late autumn.

On May 31st, the 5:00 A.M. temperature was forty-four degrees. Then the morning temperature didn't drop below fifty degrees until September 28th, when it was forty-eight degrees. According to a local weather watcher, we had seven days of temperatures of ninety degrees or above and twenty-eight days of eighty-five to eighty-nine degrees in June and July. The rest of the summer wasn't exactly frigid either.

The extremes in temperatures again showed the benefits of diversity. For grazing, the summer wasn't ideal. The cool-season grasses just sort of held their own during the heat. Some hay fields had to be grazed to make up for the shortfall in pasturage. Once the cooler days and nights of fall, along with adequate rainfall, came along, it stimulated pasture growth of the sort we've never experienced before. Here we are wintered in with two to three weeks of excellent pasture left. But as the old-timers used to say, "What you don't take off in the fall, you'll get back in the spring."

While the pasture grasses suffered in the heat, a warm-season grass, corn, loved every minute of the summer's seventy plus degree nights. For whatever reasons besides the heat and the dry June, it was a perfect growing season for corn in our community.

All summer the corn crop looked promising, but we didn't realize how promising until the grain harvest began in one of the nicest autumns in recent memory. I'll try to be modest here—but I do believe we harvested the best corn we've ever grown. The final report from the Ohio Agricultural Research and Development Center isn't in yet (they are doing a yield check), but according to our crib capacity it has to be well over two hundred bushels per acre.

What I really like is the amount of "inputs" that went into growing the crop—in the neighborhood of $30.00 to $33.00 per acre for 27,000 kernels of untreated seed corn. That's it. No commercial fertilizer, no insecticides, no herbicides. A little grease on the wheel bearings of the Pioneer plow, the corn planter, and the I&J cultivator, and the rest was sun power. Of course it wouldn't be right not to mention the many loads of animal manure that were spread on the field and then plowed down with the Kverneland plow. I guess I'm a farmer of the old school that still gets pleasure out of growing a good crop of corn. As a neighbor once told me, "I'd much sooner inspan the team and go to the field than grab the checkbook and head for the auction."

Coming to the end of another good farming year, we need to be mindful that many of the good things in life are mostly intangible and often impossible to measure, and among them are our families. Theodore Roosevelt said, "For unflagging interest and enjoyment, a household of children, if things go reasonably well, certainly makes all other forms of success and achievement lose their importance by comparison." As we get together for the holidays and share the bounty of the land, let's be grateful for family and friends and food.

A word of caution: With the high prices of natural gas and heating oil this winter, many families will be heating with wood for their first time. At least if the reports from the local woodstove dealer are an indicator – thirty-five wood burners sold in one day! Anyway, while smoke and heat detectors are always important to have in homes, they are crucial when heating with wood. Call your local fire chief for recommendations and then install alarms. And for you with systems in place, make sure the batteries are up to date. Then enjoy your woodstove, the finest heat to be had.

Blessings to all you gentle-folk.

(2005)

Bur Oak

I like trees because they seem more designed to the way they have
to live than other things do.

—Willa Cather

The only bur oak on our farm succumbed to the Christmas 2004 ice storm. A few days after the storm, I saw that it was down, but it was only this morning, when I was on my way to get a load of firewood, that I walked up the small feeder stream to check out the old oak.

The oak was rooted on the west bank of the little creek that has its origins at Al's spring-fed stock trough a mile up the hollow. Floodwaters over the years had undermined its roots until it leaned out across the stream into the pasture field. After every flood it leaned a bit more. The tons of ice that accumulated on the branches of the oak's large crown during the storm were too much and it crashed to the ground.

In this part of Ohio, where the eastern woodlands give way to the grasslands of the Midwest, the bur oak is usually a loner growing in moist well-drained floodplains. Many timber cutters call them "swamp oaks" and are unaware they cut down a bur oak. It is one of the minor oak species, alone with the shingle, scarlet, and swamp white oaks, in woodlots of predominantly white and red oaks.

What makes the bur oak interesting to me is its unique acorn. The largest of all acorns, it can measure up to two inches across and is almost enclosed by its fringed cap, giving the appearance of a human face encircled with a tightly-drawn fur-trimmed parka. Because of its fringed acorn, it is sometimes called mossycup oak. Our children called them the hippie acorns, because of that mop-top.

While the bur oak is uncommon in the East, it is the tree of the "oak openings" and the oak that colonized the prairies. Until the coming of the Europeans, the eastern woodlands had difficulty in invading the thick grasslands of the prairies, although in the continuing cycles of droughts and wet years, most of the prairies of Ohio, Indiana, and Michigan were engulfed with forestlands before the arrival of the settlers.

In *Where the Sky Began*, John Madson writes on the westward march of the eastern hardwoods: "But the grasslands had a powerful ally – a ravaging force against which most trees could not hold their prairie gains. Some of the plains Indians called it 'Red Buffalo.' The white man called it many things. It was wildfire."

Wildfires, usually started by lightning in the sun-parched tall grasses, raged across the prairies with walls of flame forty feet high and traveled at the speed of the wind. Driven by the prevailing westerly winds, the fires flew into the face of the advancing hardwoods. The woody plants could not withstand the four-hundred degrees Fahrenheit wind-driven heat and died, allowing the prairie's fire-tolerant grasses to regain lost ground.

Before the bur oaks could gain a toehold on the prairie, the way was opened by the sumac, wild plums, and other shrubs. The edge of this shrub zone may have advanced only ten feet before being driven back by fire. In the weakened area of burned brush, the bur oak set down its roots. The tough oak seedling sends down its ten-inch taproot before any leaves appear. By its third summer, the bur oak is still a three-foot sapling, but its roots will have colonized an area four feet wide and six feet down.

If the bur oak is fortunate enough to escape a wildfire for a decade, it will thrive, because by then it has grown a thick crust of corky bark and practically becomes fireproof. It is the only tree that can survive a prairie fire. With its burly fire-resistance, the bur oak slowly moved westward.

But what really set the stage for westward migration of the bur oaks was the arrival of European settlers. As soon as enough of the grasslands were plowed to stop the wildfires, bur oaks – and other hardwoods for that matter – traveled west with settlement. Aldo Leopold writes in *A Sand County Almanac* that all the bur oaks in which he counted the growth rings, except a few old veterans, dated to the 1850s and 1860s, the time that prairie wildfires ended in Wisconsin.

I don't know how old our bur oak is, but I'm guessing in the neighborhood of a hundred years. I plan to count the rings when we cut it for firewood. Next winter's heat was a long time coming and we'll savor and cherish every minute of it.

Spring

Things tend to balance out, as they say. Following a cold December we had an unusually mild January, and now as we are heading toward spring it is cold again; winter is hanging on like a terrier on a rat. But it is nice to have the ground frozen to get some late firewood cutting done and some barn animals lowered to a more manageable level.

Furthermore, I did something this winter that I had never done before—unloaded manure with a new manure spreader. As Leroy Kuhns, who also purchased a new one this winter, said, "For most of us farmers, that's a once in a lifetime event."

For those of us who use ground-driven spreaders, finding good used ones is becoming a problem. Fortunately, a number of small-scale manufacturers of both two-wheeled and four-wheeled spreaders are springing up to fill that void. One of the manufacturers repaired and reconditioned used spreaders for sixteen years before he started making new ones. He was fully aware of all the weak points of New Idea's products, so in many ways the new spreaders are improvements over the models they are replacing. Almost all the chains are now rollers and won't fly off at the slightest whim. The floor is some kind of rubberized tongue and groove that doesn't rot or rust and cleans like linoleum. The grease fittings are accessible and you don't have to slide and crawl underneath the spreader in snow or mud to do the greasing.

In small-scale farming communities, companies that manufacture equipment such as plows, spreaders, harrows, wagons, power units, and replacement parts are crucial. So are the used parts dealers. Recently I was at Midway Repair Shop getting information for Asa Chester, when a farmer stopped in carrying a large broken u-bolt from a Rosenthal corn husker. "Danny, do you have something like this?" he asked. "There should be one out in the used machinery lot." As the farmer left, Danny shouted after him, "Go through the basement and take wrenches along. That way you have to make only one trip." All the while Danny was telling me about the wood thrush that was at their bird feeder until the last day in November. One more day and it would have been a state record.

In my opinion, Midway Repair Shop in the northern part of our area and E-M Equipment in the southern end are much more important to the well-being of our community than any of the corporate box stores. Where else can one find plowshares of all kinds, walking plow landsides, jointer points, new handles for plows and seats and levers and bearings and mower parts and pitmans and binder webs and an almost new two-way plow (not for sale)? Not at Sam's Club.

Europe is also a supplier of small-scale agricultural technology: Kverneland plows from Norway, sickle mowers from Italy, and scythes from Austria, and the list could go on. Speaking of scythes … when the Swiss Anabaptists left the Bernese Oberland because of religious persecution and, on the invitation of large estate owners, moved north to the Alsace region following the Thirty Years War and the Treaty of Westphalia (1648), they left mountainous grazing land and went to land that was tilled and cropped with cereal grains. Since they were a cow-culture people, the Anabaptists soon turned some of those tilled fields into improved meadows using newly-introduced clovers and grasses, much to the ridicule of the local farmers. The introduction of legumes ended the practice of leaving a field fallow every third year.

With the improved meadows, there was at last surplus forage that could be cut and dried as hay. In order to speed up the cutting of larger tracts of hay, the scythe was introduced to replace the hand sickle—a transition that was again ridiculed and resisted by the local farmers. The locals did not accept the scythe for over one hundred years! In the early 1900s, communistic Russia was still intrigued with the hand sickle. I'm intrigued with the scythe.

(2006)

In Praise of Fencerows

Dividing our farm from the farm east of us is a fence; or, perhaps I should say, the remnant of a woven-wire fence held up by a tangle of blackberries, raspberries, wild cherry trees, and a myriad of "weeds." This fencerow is unkempt and neglected, but it abounds with wild things. This ribbon of life exists by mutual agreement between my neighbor and myself.

Even though the fencerow abounds with activity throughout the year, the apex of its life occurs in mid to late summer with the ripening of the blackberries and wild cherries and the blooming of the goldenrod. Their abundance invites the greatest diversity of creatures, from the colorful locust borer beetles and monarch butterflies on the goldenrod, to the late-nesting goldfinches on the brambles, and the many birds and mammals feeding on the berries and cherries.

Brushy fencerows are in a sense a gift from man to nature – at least if, after the posts are dug in and the fence stapled to the posts, nature is given some free rein. Birds sitting on the fence and posts will pass undigested seeds in their droppings. Some of these seeds of blackberry, wild cherry, elderberry, bittersweet, sassafras, mulberry, and unfortunately, in some areas, multiflora rose, will take root in the loose soil around the posts and, later, in soil dug up by the woodchucks. Chipmunks scurrying along the fence will bring and bury acorns and hickory nuts, while the wind will deliver dandelion, milkweed, and thistle seeds – all ingredients for a healthy fencerow.

In the northeast corner of the field that borders the fencerow is a rock pile along with a few broken pieces of plowshares and cultivator points. Next to the rocks are some shoots of serviceberry (or Juneberry), sprouts of a tree likely planted by a bird maybe a century ago.

The serviceberry brings back memories of my boyhood and the neighbor who used to own and till the next farm. He was a farmer of the old school, intelligent, interesting, and full of wisdom, and suspicious of all the newfangled innovations in agriculture. For years he farmed with a Fordson tractor and a team, then finally went to a two-plow Ferguson tractor. Yet the tractor never really speeded up his life. He always had time to stop whatever he was doing in his fields for a visit with us beneath the serviceberry, a tree he loved, for it was the first to bloom in the spring.

The serviceberry blew down in the blizzard of 1978, ten years after the neighbor died. New shoots are now growing from the stump. The spring after the blizzard, a shellbark hickory sprouted several feet from the serviceberry, at the edge of the gateway between our farms, and today is at least thirty feet high. It is now bearing nuts.

The predominant tree along the fencerow, though, is the wild cherry, and, as food for wildlife, it is the most important. In late summer and early fall, many different kinds of animals feed on its abundant fruit. This includes the red foxes, raccoons, skunks, opossums, and even deer. Sometimes when hauling wood from stacked piles in late fall, we discover caches of wild cherry pits that deer mice and chipmunks have stored for the winter. Birds, likewise, relish the cherries and feed heavily on them for a month or so. We use them ourselves to make a delicious jelly.

From April through July the fencerow rings with bird song. While we were plowing alongside it this spring, several song sparrows, a pair of bluebirds, and a cardinal entertained us. The bluebird nested in a box across the gateway from the hickory. Later, in May, I spotted a Tennessee warbler and other migrants.

The most important mammal in the fencerow must be the woodchuck. With their penchant for digging burrows, the woodchucks provide homes not only for themselves, but, when abandoned, homes for many other mammals. Most skunks and many opossums and raccoons live permanently in woodchuck burrows. Red foxes will also use the woodchuck's home to raise their pups. Should a woodchuck be in the burrow in late winter when the vixen decides on a location, the hapless animal is often killed when the fox takes over the den. Once a burrow becomes flea-infested, the young foxes are moved to a new den, where, very likely, another woodchuck will be kicked out.

Cottontails, too, and even pheasants and bobwhites will, in severe weather, seek the safety of a woodchuck hole.

Woodchucks do, however, eat hay crops, soybeans, garden vegetables, and sometimes, young corn plants, and so they are despised by many farmers and gardeners. Thousands are shot each year by varmint hunters. But in spite of persecution by dogs, foxes, and hunters, this hearty animal is thriving. Last summer when I cut the first round of oats I found four new burrows. As long as there are fencerows, there will be woodchucks.

Fencerows often serve as travel lines for animals, especially deer and foxes, and on hillsides, fencerows help to control erosion. Many fields on the uphill side of a fencerow are a foot or more higher than the field on the downhill side. Another benefit of the fencerow is that it is a renewable source of heat for the winter months. In a year or so the bigger trees in our fencerow can be cut and sawed into stove-lengths. For a fast-growing tree, seasoned cherry is surprisingly good firewood. The wild cherry stumps will quickly sprout shoots, growing sometimes six to eight feet in the first year, and the cycle will be repeated about every ten years. Cutting some of the trees will not greatly harm the value of the fencerow for wildlife, particularly if the brush is left in piles for additional cover.

Sadly, fencerows have become unfashionable. They began disappearing when the bulldozer became affordable, farm size increased, and the 2,4-D brush killers were developed. Weed killers and clean mowing invites fescue to take over and the fencerow becomes a biological desert. Soon after the demise of the fencerow, hunters began complaining about the scarcity of rabbits and pheasants. The blame was mistakenly put on the fox and the owl.

When we consider tearing out the fencerow, we think of the buck rubs, then the fox den, and the covey of quail, the serviceberry ... bulldozing this ribbon of life definitely wouldn't be "cost effective." Too much would be lost.

Summer

While moving the fence for the dairy cows this morning I reflected on the advances electric fencing has made the past three or four decades. In my early teenaged years I would go with my dad to the woods and help him cut down three-inch thick ironwood trees. We then sawed them in forty-inch lengths, sharpened one end, pounded it six inches into the ground, nailed a ceramic insulator to the top, wired on the fence, and we had electric fencing.

It was the technology of the day and it worked quite well. Needless to say, we didn't move the fence after every milking. We would graze six-acre fields for up to a week or two, usually second or third cutting hay, or the new hay seeding that followed wheat.

Soon after my wife and I started farming we purchased smooth steel rod posts with a triangular plate about six inches up from the bottom for added stability. A heavy hammer was needed to pound them into the ground. The insulators were black plastic with an eyebolt and wing nut to attach it to the post. But the wire snapped into a notch on the insulator. It was a great improvement in technology.

Next on the scene were the yellow plastic insulators that had an attached plastic nut to fasten it to the steel post. Another improvement. That is, until the white-tailed deer population began to increase and rutting bucks hitting the fence would send those yellow insulators into the next field. I still occasionally unearth one of the plastic artifacts.

Then about fifteen years ago we got our first step-in plastic posts and poly wire. I still marvel over that great leap forward in appropriate technology. I'll probably never get over it just like my dad never quite got over the marvel of twine knotters on the binder and hay baler. "A mechanical device that ties a knot just the way a human hand does," he would say with admiration.

Poly wire gave us the flexibility to successfully cross-fence for the first time. I had tried it with wire and such a mess of kinks resulted, and broken wire afterward, that I soon gave up on it. Improved New Zealand twelve-volt fence chargers also arrived and I thereby quit moving fence with the charger on like I could with the American-made fencers.

For a long time I thought it would be nice to have a remote shutoff for the fence charger for those times I'm at the back part of the farm and forgot to shut off the charger. Instead of walking or biking home to switch it off one would merely use the remote controller, punch the "off" button, move the fence, and hit the "on" button. I hear they are now available – $80.00.

There has been a lot of discussion on the National Animal Identification System (NAIS) that is scheduled to be implemented by the USDA in the next two or three years. It supposedly is to protect us from Mad Cow disease and Avian flu and every person who owns even one horse, cow, pig, chicken, sheep, pigeon, goldfish, canary, or any other livestock will be forced to register their home, including owner's name, address, and telephone number, and keyed to Global Positioning System coordinates for satellite monitoring, in a giant federal database under a seven-digit "premises ID number."

Forgive me, but Mark Twain's wisdom comes to mind, "Sometimes I wonder whether the world is being run by smart people who are putting us on, or by imbeciles who really mean it." I'm not too worried about it because I think it will be too cumbersome and expensive for them to administer. Forcing half a million farmers into compliance will be as tough as getting those Afghan farmers to quit growing poppies. With one out of thirty-two people in this country already in prison, there may be no room for all of us.

(2006)

Fall

I tend to forget how much I enjoy autumn until it arrives again. We're here in the best part of summer, late summer and that long, lovely passage into fall. The roadsides are aglow with goldenrod and asters, bees are gathering late nectar; our summer resident squirrels left last week for cold season homes, and the cows are contented on pastures that are still the sweetness of a green world, and where the flies are greatly diminished with the cooling of the earth.

Turkey vultures are drifting southward but are in no great hurry to reach their destination. The big birds are always in the mood for a warm meal. The other night—it happens four or five times during the course of the summer—an opossum took a shortcut across our lawn and the dog got him. The dog is wise to "possum-acting" and calls their bluff. Anyhow, the down-on-his-luck animal hitched a ride to the field on the manure spreader and when I returned with the next load, a vulture was already dining on the opossum. The following load there were two vultures, but they were about twenty feet from the carcass, as a red-tailed hawk had claimed the dinner and between bites, would, with hackles raised, stare down the vultures.

Here in summer-turning-to-fall, we also have some of the finest eating of the year for us—the last of the sweet corn, endless vine-ripened tomatoes dripping with juice and flavor, green beans, new potatoes, early apples and pumpkin pie – the list could go on and on. A fine time of the year.

As the year winds down to the ripening of the corn and a possible late hay cutting, we can summarize the growing season and conclude that it was good, though a bit on the wet side here in Ohio. My neighbor, whose farm is well drained, told me yesterday that their corn may even beat last year's record crop. My expectations are a little lower, but nevertheless, still an excellent crop. We are well off with hay and grain for the winter, while the woodpile needs work. The summer's storm took down a three-hundred-year-old white oak and some smaller trees in our woods, so now all we need are several days and we'll be really set for the cold months.

The down side of the year is the low milk prices. It's tough on young farmers who have to buy feed with the price of milk at record lows. Pete Harden (*The Milkweed*) sees an improvement in price for the late fall and early winter.

The asinine National Animal Identification System (NAIS) is still cooking, although I was told recently that the USDA has put everything on the back burner for now. Whether it is for real or an election day smoke screen, I don't know. Our own congressman has more than enough troubles of his own, so he pays little attention to NAIS. If you have access to *Rural Heritage*, please read the roster on how Congress voted on an amendment to the 2007 Farm Bill to stop funding for NAIS. Only thirty-four out of 435 voted to starve the beast. The Farm Bureau is in favor of NAIS. For food security, they claim. The fear factor at work.

I came across this quote by George Gerbner, who headed the Annenberg School for Communication for twenty-five years: "Fearful people are more dependent, more easily manipulated and controlled, more susceptible to deceptively simple, strong, tough measures and hard-line postures. … They may accept and even welcome repression if it promises to relieve their insecurities."

Maybe we are as the Grand Inquisitor said in Dostoevsky's *The Brothers Karamazov*, "We will be your slaves, but feed us."

As our families gather around the home table on Thanksgiving Day, let's remember that we plant, but God gives the increase, and then we harvest. Blessings.

(2006)

Migration

Cold weather has arrived. Yesterday and today the temperature never topped the freezing point and there was a brisk wind to boot; a wind that sliced right through denim and flannel. The arctic blast brought some interesting migrants to the cornfields. My grandson and I were watching a flock of Canada geese overhead when we noticed one goose just a shade smaller and, besides, it had a white neck and head—the blue phase of the snow goose.

Later today, when the geese returned to the pond for rest and safety, three more "blues" had joined the flock of several hundred birds. These three were immatures and appeared charcoal gray all over. We were delighted. It's been a number of years since snow geese visited our fields.

This past fall was an interesting time for southward migrating birds here on our farm. When I mowed our last hay of the season, the third cutting of a new seeding, a northern harrier hung around all the while I was mowing in our far field. Every year I see migrating harriers, but they are five-minute sightings and then the hawk is gone. This one hunted all afternoon, low over the fields, to occasionally turn sharply and drop for a mouse and then perch on the ground to eat the plump meadow vole. The hawk was an adult female with brownish plumage. All harriers have a prominent white rump, which is readily visible when the raptor is coursing low over fields, as this one was.

While the harrier was mousing next door, I flushed a Virginia rail from in front of the mowing machine. A real skulker, the rail flew only a short distance and dropped back into the unmowed part of the field. I could see the grasses stir as the rail moved ahead of me, but it refused to fly until the last round and then only to the nearest cover. This rail was surely migrating and may have flown hundreds of miles before stopping in our hay field for food and rest. But it definitely wasn't ready to move on yet. It always astounds me that rails even bother to migrate, as weak as their flight appears to be. But then, if the monarch can migrate several thousand miles to Mexico, the rails can surely make it to the marshes and bayous of the Gulf Coast. Maybe the rail was waiting for the hurricane season to end before venturing farther south.

The most bizarre event of the fall migration for us involved a gaggle of turkey vultures. Those big carrion-eaters loaf their way south during the halcyon days of autumn and they are always on the make for a free lunch. We had a Jersey cow calve at the opposite end of the farm from the harrier's field, down by the woods and creek and brier patches and Carolina wrens–well secluded–a perfect place for a bovine birthing. Unfortunately, the calf was born dead.

Emily checked the cow in the evening and took some grain along for her. Already the vultures were congregating low in the trees around the cow and calf. She claimed there were at least forty of the spooky birds in the gathering dusk. How did the word spread? There was no odor because the weather was cool. Have the buzzards someway tied into cell phone technology?

The cow was brought home, and on the second morning, which was foggy, as I walked past the birthing place, I was startled by a swoosh of big wings lifting heavy birds. I'm not easily unnerved, but I'll confess this came close, as the dew-laden vultures labored to the nearest trees. One small tree harbored seventeen of the somber birds. On checking the calf, I could see their problem; in the chillness of autumn the calf "ripened" slowly and only the delicate parts had been eaten. I will skip the details. Even the biggest, toughest buzzard, the one that was always perched on the carcass–surely the alpha bird of the bunch–was unable to break the skin. By the end of the week, they had found a way and the vultures had eaten and were gone.

The migrants here now, besides the geese, are the American pipits and horned larks and rough-legged hawks. All enjoy the open spaces of the fields. The feeder birds will be here any day. I have seen a red-breasted nuthatch and a few dark-eyed juncos. The tree sparrows will surely follow.

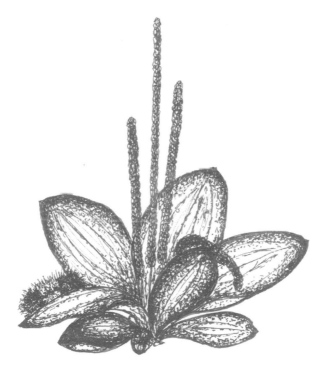

Winter

Good-by, kind year, we walk no more together,
But here in kind happiness we part.

—Sarah Doudney

There is almost no richer gift to farmers in the northern latitudes than a nice prolonged late autumn Indian summer. We are nearing the end of such a one right now. It gave us time to get the corn harvested, firewood in, and an overall preparedness for the coming winter season; all in the comfort of fifty to sixty degree temperatures.

Likewise, the pleasant and dry weather allowed us to graze some new grass seedings without tearing up the fields. When we started dairying in the late 1960s, our on-grass/off-grass seasons were almost evenly split between six months indoors and six months outdoors. A few times we grazed until Thanksgiving Day, but as a rule the cows were inside on stored feed by November 15th. Now it is closer to seven-and-a-half months on grass and four-and-a-half months indoors.

But the signs for a weather change are everywhere, including this morning's weather map. A massive trough of cold reaching all the way from Alaska to Oklahoma and then northeast across the eastern Great Lakes region is approaching. Kansas has snow and Wisconsin thundershowers. It appears we are in for an early-season Alberta Clipper.

This forenoon as I walked to the back of the farm to short-fence one of the pastures, a flock of horned larks took wing. In spite of the wind-driven pelting rain, the seventy-five or so birds seemed exuberant as they wheeled about and chased each other across the field. Flying a large circle, they came back to land where they had taken off.

As the cold season progresses, more horned larks will be joining the birds here on the farm and will stay until late February before dispersing northward. The larks are seed eaters and that means they go for cracked corn, which we spread for them after the first significant snowfall. Nothing fancy, simply whole ear corn ground for the cows. The larks don't eat the tiny bits of cob meal. The grit for their gizzards they find along the edge of the county road after the crew has plowed and salted the road free of snow.

In harsh winters, snow buntings, and some Lapland longspurs, can swell the flock of larks to hundreds of birds that eat five gallons or more of grain a day. But as soon as the snow melts, the flock disperses down to the faithful horned larks again. Unlike feeder birds such as the cardinals, chickadees, and titmice, who will frequent sunflower-stocked feeders in spite of the weather conditions, horned larks prefer to find their own food.

December a year ago was below average cold and the horned larks dined on cow feed daily. But after New Year's Day the weather moderated and stayed mild until spring and the larks ignored the grain spread for them. Horned larks will feed on common ragweed seeds, also lamb's-quarter, but what they really like is to find grains in freshly spread livestock manure.

All of us that have ever walked through rural areas on the annual Christmas Bird Counts know where to look for the larks – in the fields where some diligent farmer has spread several loads of manure. Perhaps we'll pick up a few snow buntings or a longspur ...

The Alberta Clipper has arrived. The wind is roaring through the maple and I hear metal roofing flapping on the barn. That is always an ominous sound, which means tying down a ladder to keep it from blowing over, because I do need a way down from the roof. The roof has been on that part of the barn since 1925 when my uncle put it on and it has served us well. A few metal screws should give it a couple more years.

(2006)

Spring

As we approach the vernal equinox, the pulse quickens as our thoughts turn to spring and grass. This fine time of the year when the earth warms, animals return to pasture, hepatica blooms, peepers call, wood frogs cluck, and migrant birds wing northward to spend the warm seasons is with us. Is there anyone who dislikes spring? I can't imagine there is, except a crotchety curmudgeon or two.

Right now I'm pruning our fruit trees. Some are apple trees that my parents planted over sixty years ago. Most of the old orchard is gone. But four trees remain, a yellow transparent, the early apple for sauce that still ranks number one for many in our family; a Macintosh, another favorite fall apple for sauce; a Grimes golden; and a Northern Spy, the apple of all apples in my opinion, for dumplings and pies and cobblers on crisp autumn days. I hope to graft these heirloom varieties on new rootstock this spring because the four standard-sized trees are reaching the end of their productive lives.

We also added to the orchard in the decades since we started farming. Thus we have both yellow and red delicious, gala, mutzu, and some others. All of our plantings have been on dwarf or semi-dwarf rootstock. While the smaller trees bear fruit sooner, they lack the longevity of the old standard trees.

Pruning trees on a sixty-degree March day is pure bliss. Working in the young world of early spring, shirtsleeves rolled up and loppers in hand, I am there to observe the changes each new day brings. Our eastern meadowlarks, while a few were around all winter, are now singing *Spring-of-the-year-is-here!* with gusto.

The cottontails are venturing away from the brushpile for longer periods of time and a few females may already have young in well-hidden nests piled with rabbit fur. The great-horned owls are feeding young and are waiting for the cottontails to leave their nest. Over-wintering butterflies – the mourning cloak and Milbert's tortoiseshell – are out and about, as are the wooly bear caterpillars and the honeybees.

I checked the bees and they are well. Last fall, in spite of the poor honey crop, I removed one shallow super of honey from the hive for our use. Several days later I had a change of heart and returned the honey to the bees. That is what they are feeding on now and I'm sure it saved the colony during the late harsh winter. The bees were requeened in late summer and the young queen kept on laying into late fall and the colony entered the winter much too strong and naturally consumed a lot of honey over the winter. The table honey we sacrificed last year should be returned this year.

This is the time of the year that our youngest daughter and I liked to "walk" the creek looking for treasures. The winter floods created new sand and gravel bars and we loved combing those deposits for Indian artifacts, old bottles, mason jars, bones, shoes, teeth, or whatever. Emily still has boxes of "treasures" she found over the years. On the sand bars were the tracks of the mink and raccoon and muskrat. Along the sandy bottom of the deeper pools was the single track of the fresh water mussel. All children should have a creek winding through their childhood.

NAIS just doesn't want to die. It seems the USDA has passed the ball to the states. Farmers in Ohio received letters with an application form for ID-ing their farms. Every farmer I talked to got some additional BTUs out of it.

May the days be pleasant and the rains gentle as we behold the unfolding of the season.

(2007)

Early Flowers

A friend wrote and said her snowdrops are blooming. Since we don't have snowdrops, our claim to an early flower right now is the lowly skunk cabbage. The plump spadix within the hood, or spathe, of the skunk cabbage is covered with small yellow flowers that, with their rotten flesh scent, attract insects when the daytime temperature climbs to the fifties. Not showy, but a flower nevertheless.

As spring progresses, more showy wildflowers begin to appear. One of the first ones is coltsfoot. A favorite of mine, coltsfoot with its bright yellow dandelion-like flowers blooms along roadsides and on ditch banks. Perhaps because it grows in such inhospitable conditions is why I like it so much. Pushing their reddish-green scaly stalks up through gravel and the winter's accumulation of soggy litter, the bright flowers vividly announce spring for all to see.

Between our house and the country school our children attended is a nice colony of coltsfoot. As soon as they burst into bloom on the east-facing ditch bank, a small hand carried home a bouquet to grace the center of our kitchen table.

Coltsfoot is one of those plants that field guides list as "naturalized," meaning it was brought to New England by early colonists from Europe and then escaped the gardens and traveled west. Many plants were brought along for garden flowers and others for their medicinal values. Coltsfoot was one that fit both categories. Its early yellow blossoms added cheer to the settlers' spring season, but it also served as a "cough dispeller."

Herbalists as far back as Pliny regarded coltsfoot as the best herb for lung and thoracic problems. A tea made from boiling the leaves in water and sweetening with honey was recommended for colds and asthma. The old herbalists, however, usually smoked the dried leaves of coltsfoot to capture its lung-healing values.

The leaves of coltsfoot are where the plant gets its name. After the yellow flowers have bloomed and gone to seed is when the leaves begin to appear in the shape of a colt's foot. (Its fluffy seed heads are similar to those of the dandelion). By early summer, they are the size of the feet of a Percheron two-year-old.

Another early spring wildflower that blooms before its leaves show any sign of life is the hepatica, or liverwort. Hepatica comes in two varieties—the round-lobed and sharp-lobed. The ones I usually come across are the sharp-lobed hepatica. Since the beautiful whitish-lavender to pale purple flowers open so early, I often miss their peak bloom. In this part of Ohio, the delicate flowers that open on the tops of three- to four-inch hairy stems appear in the first half of April. Spring plowing and birding are more compatible than plowing and botanizing.

For that reason, I transplanted five hepatica plants to our woods, hoping to daily chart their course as they pushed up through the winter-worn leaves and unfolded their blossoms to the warmth of the spring sun. It was a mistake. Over a period of six years, fewer flowers opened and then on the seventh spring, none appeared. I now regret uprooting those five hepaticas and transplanting them to a soil for which they weren't suited.

While the coltsfoot and hepatica brave the edge of winter to show off their beauty, in several weeks the woodlands will be liberally covered with anemone, Spring beauties, bloodroot, violets and trout lilies, trillium and toadshade, and harbinger-of-spring. All of these, plus the crocuses and daffodils in our yard, have medicinal properties. They purge the winter melancholia.

September

September's Baccalaureate
A combination is
Of crickets—crows—and Retrospects
And a dissembling Breeze

That hints without assuming —
An Innuendo sear
That makes the Heart put up its Fun
And turn Philosopher.
                              —Emily Dickinson

September brings a whisper of autumn; a time of slowing down and the beginning of color, and silo filling. September should be a season instead of a month. The early morning eastern sky is dominated by Orion, the mighty hunter. And Sirius, the bright Dog Star is again shimmering low in the southeast. For six weeks during midsummer, Sirius rises and sets with the sun and is not visible.

Traditionally, the September full moon has been called the Harvest Moon because it gives farmers an extra hour or two of working time (we don't really need it). The Harvest full moon is on the twenty-first and the autumnal equinox occurs in the early morning of the 23rd, the time when the noon sun is straight above the equator and day and night is of equal duration and it officially marks the beginning of fall. Although the moon will rise fifty and one-half minutes later each evening, for several nights following its full phase the moon will appear big and brilliant as it rises in the east.

It is here in the closing days of summer that the flowering of life reaches its full abundance. Unmowed meadows are flush with the purple flowers of New York ironweed and the yellow-flowering wingstem. The first big New England asters are opening. The less showy white asters and bluish heart-leaved asters and goldenrods are everywhere – along roadsides and in fencerows, in wet fields and along woods' edges. Swamp milkweeds in wetlands are producing a late crop of monarchs. While the buzz of a mosquito near our ear gives us pause this year, the flight of butterflies gives us hope. Almost without fail, the first monarch of the season arrives here the first week of June. This year it wasn't until the end of June that the first migrants arrived. And it wasn't until late summer that they became common.

Redtails cry from high in the cerulean sky and I worry because West Nile Virus is killing many raptors. Red-tailed hawks and great horned owls, especially, are being hit hard by the insidious disease. While birdsong is diminishing – occasionally a song sparrow bursts forth in song but stops short as if he made a mistake – insect songs abound. The fencerows and gardens are ringing with the crisp stridulations of grasshoppers and crickets … a constant buzzing and rasping and scratching that continues throughout the days and nights until a hard frost ends the chorus.

Well-worn trails lead from burrows in the fencerows to the hayfields where groundhogs travel daily to pig-out on alfalfa and clover. After a summer of digging new burrows and dodging bullets, the groundhogs are now laying on fat for the coming cold months of hibernation. Right now, life for the grizzled rodent consists of eating and sleeping and keeping an eye out for the dogs. Foraging skunks worry little about the dogs, but opossums should. In the past week, two possums crossed our lawn during the night and didn't make it. The dogs presented me with their "gift" as soon as I left the house for the morning chores.

In the woodlands, squirrels are feeding on hickory and beechnuts. The coons are finishing off the last sweet corn. White oak acorns are beginning to drop and the deer are finding them.

Yesterday I checked a bluebird house and already a family of white-footed mice had moved in and settled down for the winter. The bluebirds have other boxes for shelter so I left the family of mice for now.

Late-summer-turning-to-autumn is also when the gardens and orchards yield some of their finest bounty—late sweet corn, tomatoes, peppers, potatoes, cucumbers, beets, and elderberries that can be prepared in countless ways. This is the time when canning, preserving, and freezing reaches its peak. Dozens of relishes, sauces, pickles, and jellies are put up for the winter. From the orchard come late peaches and fresh McIntosh and Northern Spy apples for dumplings and sauce and pies.

And perhaps best of all, several good rains have pastures growing again. Moving fence in the early morning beneath reclining Orion, walking in grasses and legumes halfway up my gum boots, is pleasure at its best.

Poets call autumn the melancholy season, but as a farmer I can't see anything sad about this time of the year. My feelings for September are like my friend's are for pies—he's never seen one he didn't like.

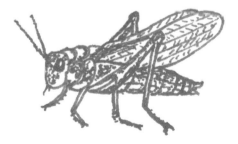

Fall

One of the many benefits of being a dairy farmer is that you rise early and get to see the morning sky. To my way of thinking, late summer and early autumn's night sky is the finest of the year. Orion the mighty hunter is slowing getting to his feet and Sirius, after an absence of six weeks during the Dog days, is again clearly visible. Right now, Venus is the bright morning star and the planet of love simply sparkles in the east here during the new moon.

As I go back the field lane to move fence, birds that spent the night blended in with its dust and gravel take wing. The usual birds are savannah and vesper sparrows, water pipits, and horned larks. This past week I flushed out a shorebird, likely a yellowlegs, and a common nighthawk that had sought out the dryness of the lane for a night's rest.

An obvious truth is that summer is over, and an indicator of seasonal change is the nighthawk migration. Since the long-winged birds depend entirely on flying insects for food, they move south as the temperatures drop in the northern states. On one or two evenings in early September we are treated to the annual spectacle of the southward flight of nighthawks as they seine the air for insects. Nighthawks are easy to identify by the broad white bars across their slender wings.

Most of our common summer birds have gone the way of the nighthawks: the swallows (of the four species on the farm, the barn swallows were the last to depart), the house wrens, orchard and Baltimore orioles, and the bobolinks. Even the dooryard robins are gone. If it weren't for the singing insects, it would be too quiet around here. We did have two new birds nesting in our yard this summer; the red-headed woodpecker and yellow-billed cuckoo. The shy cuckoos are still around here at the autumnal equinox because we hear their *ka-ka-ka-ka-kowlp-kowlp* calls. The red-headed woodpeckers have moved to the woods, but visit the corncrib regularly. They will likely stay around all winter if the corn supply holds out.

For a while in late spring and early summer, it appeared bleak that we farmers would have an adequate supply of winter feed. In our four decades of dairying, we had never experienced a spring like this past one. Late March brought a period of unusually warm weather and pastures and hayfields responded with early growth. We turned the cows out to pasture, two to three weeks earlier than normally, even though we knew that it was too warm for too long, too early.

April then evened the score as temperatures dropped to the mid-teens, and as a result the pastures never burst forth into a spring flush. First cutting hay was short, and second cutting hay was an exercise in futility. We had to graze all except eleven acres of what would have been second cutting hay and that field made 150 small square bales. Not per acre – total.

Naturally, hay prices skyrocketed as did grain prices as farmers scrambled for feed. Then tropical storm Erin hit Texas, curved northeast and showered us with three-and-a-half inches of gentle rain. The crops responded in kind and third and fourth cuttings of hay produced as much as the first cutting. As a rule, first cutting hay provides sixty percent of the hay crop in this part of the country. Most farmers are now set for the winter with forages. In spite of the drought, the corn crop looks like another crib buster and we have autumn pastures way beyond our highest hopes. Now we can focus on the woodpile and enjoy this golden season. I wish September had sixty days.

On behalf of everybody here, may your Thanksgiving Day be filled with love and family.

(2007)

On Grass and Related Matters

One day in the spring of 1883, as a Scandinavian farmer, John Christiansen, was plowing his fields in North Dakota, he looked up to find that he was being watched by an old and solemn Lakota Sioux.

Silently the old native watched as the dark soil furled up and the prairie grass was turned under. Christiansen stopped, leaned against the handle of the plow, pushed his Stetson back on his head, and rolled a cigarette. He watched amusedly as the old man knelt, thrust his fingers into the mat of root-bound soil, measured the depth of the furrow, fingered the sod and buried grass.

Then the old Sioux straightened up and looked at the farmer.

"Wrong side up," he said and walked away.

For many years this story was regarded as funny as it supposedly revealed the ignorance of the old Indian. But time has a way of flipping the tables – the old Lakota was onto something. Grass has its virtues, especially in dairy.

In 1949, Louis Bromfield wrote that grass farming was spreading like a wildfire in the great Midland of our country, at the very heart of the Corn Belt. Unfortunately, in the following quarter century the wildfire was extinguished. The nation's dairy farmers became more mechanized and cheap fossil fuel dependent, and evolved into corn/alfalfa confinement dairy farmers. The grasslands again became wrong side up.

Now grass is back, and growing. We began systematic grass farming a decade ago when we began to make some grass seedings more directed toward grazing than for hay. Although we had been rotational grazing for many years, it was in bluegrass/white clover pastures, and in hayfields of red clover/alfalfa/timothy. Because we were organic, more emphasis was put on orchard grass than on the ryegrasses, since the ryegrasses require higher levels of nitrogen. It has worked well.

I am not a scientist, nor do I pretend to be one. I am merely an observer and what I see happening on our farm with organic grazing pleases me.

When we switched to organic dairying, I had a short list of concerns in the catacombs of my mind. Besides nitrogen of course, I worried about Canada thistles and quack grass in the twenty acres of corn and twelve acres of oats that we grow. To my surprise, both have practically disappeared on our farm. I'm not sure why, but I note that rotationally intensive grazing helped a great deal in eliminating the pest plants.

Likewise with nitrogen; it was not the problem I feared. We have access to a quantity of composted broiler manure from a neighboring poultry house, which supplies some nitrogen for the grass fields. The rest is furnished by the legumes and the manure from the dairy herd.

Once the organic matter and calcium, potassium, phosphorus, and nitrogen have the right balance in the soil, it results in growth and health of plants, animals, and people. Looking back over the past decade, our herd health has improved considerably. Mastitis is only a rare occurrence and in that period only one freshening cow retained her placenta, which she then released within five days. It has been said that grass is the Great Healer and I believe it; both for animals and for the soil.

Starting in mid-April, the herd is grazed on large plots of four to twelve acres and as grass growth increases, the paddock size is reduced to less than half an acre every twelve hours. This year, since late May, the herd of thirty-five Jerseys, one bull and one steer, has gotten ninety percent of their grazing forage from eighteen acres. Of course, it has been a great year for grazing here in Ohio. But so have been the past three years.

Our standard seed mixture for pasture is (per acre) five pounds of Baraula orchard grass (Barenbrug), five pounds of improved timothy such as Barliza or Sunrise, five pounds of a perennial ryegrass, five pounds of multiple-year medium red clover, eight pounds of alfalfa, and two pounds of Alice white clover. On fields at the far end of the farm that are difficult to graze, the ryegrass and Alice white clover are dropped from the mixture. Both are tough to dry for hay, so more alfalfa and red clover are added.

As a rule, our new grass seedings are made in the springtime with oats as a cover crop. The oats are then harvested for grain. We made our first ever fall grass seeding this year. The following day it rained an inch. Perfect. Next spring we'll find out whether it worked.

So far I have celebrated the merits of grazing that relate to agriculture, nutrition, and health. Now for some other benefits: first, economics, which won't take long. It's profitable. Our purchased feed costs usually run under $4000 a year. We do feed hay during the grazing year and the cows eat about one 4x4 round bale a month. They get ten pounds of home-grown ground ear corn and oats daily; plus the herd gets free choice kelp, Redmond salt, and sodium bicarbonate.

Another benefit, and the last one I'll mention, is moving the fence every twelve hours. That's my assignment. While our daughter and son-in-law milk, I move the fence. Every evening and morning at 4:30 to 5:00 it gets me to the fields, and what a pleasure it is to see the "other" life on the farm. Meteors slice through the sky. Great-horned and barn owls call, roosters crow. The eyes of a red fox – a pair raised a family along the line fence – cross the beam of my light.

The evening fence moving is serenaded by birdsong: meadow and horned larks, bobolinks, vesper, savannah, and grasshopper sparrows. Red-tailed hawks and kestrels hunt over the pastures for organic voles. Two vultures, drifting southward for the winter, stop to dine on an opossum.

I don't like to see the grazing season end, but we aren't there yet. We're here in that fine time of the year, late summer and that long, lovely passage into autumn when the pastures are still the sweetness of a green world and the cows are fully content and producing an abundance of healthy and nutritious milk.

Winter

From some early indicators, our winter may be more severe than the previous two or three. Already in late October red-breasted nuthatches, a boreal forest species, showed up at our feeders. Last week a dark phase rough-legged hawk, another northern bird, made a visit to our fields, hunting for field mice. The hawk was as black as a turkey vulture. The first time I saw it, perched on top of a step-in fence post, I thought it was a vulture. But when it flew, its underwings showed patches of white. Although the hawk lacked the usual white rump of a roughleg, it definitely was a rough-legged hawk, a handsome one, as it flew across the field to alight in the grove of quaking aspens.

As of this writing, in early December, the dairy cows are still grazing good quality pasture. I'm sure we are nearing the end of the grazing season, which began on March 28, as winter's chill wind grips us with its icy fingers. We are starting to feed more hay and baleage and, in a day or so, we'll start feeding some corn silage. Then the barn will be fully enveloped by the wonderful aroma of winter and shared by the barn cats, dog, calves, cows, horses, and a few little brown bats.

Even in this period of transition from full pasture to barn feed, milk production remains good and so is the butterfat content. Freshly rolled oats sweetened with honey and fruit and topped with five-percent-plus butterfat milk is a breakfast supreme. That, and a cup of steaming high-octane Volcano coffee, sets the day off on its proper path.

This winter, my wife and I will celebrate our fortieth anniversary of milking cows. It would be more accurate to say that we help, because our daughter and son-in-law do the milking now. I move fences, feed hay, clean the milking area, and try to be helpful wherever I'm needed.

Reflecting on those four decades, we have seen a lot of changes in the dairy industry across the nation. In that span, thousands of small farms disappeared and markets changed. My dad shipped milk to a small cooperative, which evolved into a larger one and finally merged with other larger co-ops until our milk check was being mailed from Kansas City. About that time a local dairy processor decided to quit buying their milk from the mega-cooperative and buy directly from local farms. We switched and were well pleased.

For a while in the early 1960s, my dad had his Grade A dairy license revoked because he kept horses in the same barn where the cows were milked. There was a surplus of milk at the time and the state found a nifty way to eliminate hundreds of small dairy farmers from the pool by "discovering" that the horse is "bad" for milk quality. Electricity was also mandated as an absolute requirement to produce wholesome milk. More dairy farms were eliminated.

When Elsie and I took over the dairy, the state was reconsidering their dim-witted restrictions, and by 1968 we were again issued a license to market Grade A milk. One demand however–there had to be one Coleman pressure lantern for every four cows.

One thing that didn't change over those years was the quality of the milk haulers. Friendly, hardworking, and fine people, every one of them. In all kinds of weather–snow, sleet, ice–they came, and still do, to pick up our milk. At first, the can milk and then bulk, and they deliver it to the processors on time. Even on some holidays they were on duty. There was Clyde, Carl, Dutch, Raymond, Levi, Firman, Sara Ann, Roger, Dale, Jeff, Dave, the Sidle family, and now Fred. I probably missed a few, but my hat is off to you in gratitude for your dedication.

May your Christmas be filled with love and family and the New Year with blessings.

(2007)

Spring

A man's interest in a single bluebird is worth more than a complete but dry list of the fauna and flora of a town.

—Henry David Thoreau

My interest this latter part of the winter has not been on a single bluebird, but on about three or four that feed on a mixture of peanut butter and cornmeal by our kitchen window. Every day, regardless of the weather, the pleasant birds feed and sing, which adds to our viewing and listening enjoyment for the day.

The silence of winter is broken not only by the songs of the bluebirds but by other birdsong. Song sparrows, cardinals, and of course the buoyant Carolina wrens are adding their voices to the choir as spring edges northward at about fifteen to seventeen miles a day.

A friend said that he is ready for spring but not quite prepared for it yet. I could say the same. There were a number of winter projects I haven't finished. One is a series of articles on starting farming sustainably and maintaining it.

If this present farm situation of high grain prices continues we'll be in for some interesting times. Should milk prices drop to $17.00 or lower per hundredweight, many dairy farmers will be operating in the red. Corn and soybean prices are being driven by the demand for ethanol and bio-diesel, and wheat prices are at record levels.

The livestock end of agriculture has for decades depended on an abundant supply of cheap grain and now that is changing. How it will all play out remains to be seen. One thing is certain; food prices will rise. In the broad field of divergent views on our energy and economic outlook, I'm probably closer to the prophets of economic turmoil than I am to the believers that shale oil, fuel cells, ethanol, bio-diesel, and the Goddess of Technology will provide and fuel another century of economic expansion.

I sense an ominous rumbling on the horizon that our addiction to economic growth is in peril and that it will force adjustments to be made in the lifestyles of many people in this nation, outside of the *nouveau riche* and the truly destitute, in the next decade. First, food and clothing. For those not growing and producing most of their own food, buying locally may become a necessity instead of a choice as the energy crisis translates into a consumer goods crisis. When the big box stores get clobbered by high transportation costs, more shopping will be done at farmers' markets, small neighborhood groceries, bulk food stores, and thrift stores.

We'll rely more on family, friends, and neighbors. We'll trade labor and food. Find out what you can get from your neighbor, and what you have to offer in return. Our rolled oats and honey for your hard winter wheat and maple syrup. A great deal of this is already being done locally.

The way we travel will also be affected. More biking, walking, car-pooling, and public transportation (if it's available) will be done. We'll do more traveling at home, which I prefer anyway. Whenever we farmers leave home for a few days there is always a lot of preparatory work—grinding enough feed for a week, making sure all the equipment is in tip-top shape—oil changed, belts tightened, pastures lined up—all to make it easier for the relief milkers. We can still do all this preparing and then stay at home. A week's holiday without travel costs. I've always wanted to do that.

(2008)

May Day

An Andrew Wyeth painting shows children, and possibly some adults if my memory serves me correctly, dancing around a Maypole in celebration of the arrival of spring. I, and most other dairy graziers in northern climes, could join in that revelry if the celebration of May Day hadn't have been declared so ideologically significant. After all, frail old Fidel celebrates it and some of us remember the former Soviet Union parading its military muscle on May Day—countless trucks laden with missiles as big as silos. So, in order to be politically correct, we farmers skip the dancing and rejoice less obviously than the folks in Wyeth's painting do. But it's a great time of the year nevertheless.

Winter was late in arriving, but when it came, the season stayed around for a while. At least long enough that we greeted the arrival of spring with joy. The grime and lifeless litter of winter was finally washed away with a robust thundershower and overnight a patina of green appeared on the fields. With it came the confidence and hope of another growing season.

Subtle signs of spring had begun appearing in late winter already—the call of the great horned owl booming from the woodlot in the early morning, horned larks nesting in mid-March, skunk cabbage pushing its hood up through icy meadow bogs, skeins of tundra swans flying north. But it wasn't until the spring peepers and wood frogs began their mating chorus in early April that we began to seriously think spring.

March and April are the promise and May the fulfillment. In more years than not in this part of the country, May 1st marks the arrival of the Baltimore oriole. The brilliant orange and white and black male claims the maple tree in our front yard as his home turf and he makes music all the day long. While the peak of the great northward migration of neo-tropical birds such as the wood warblers is still ten days to two weeks away, our summer resident birds are by now staking out their territories.

The bobolinks made their appearance in the pastures and hayfields the last week in April. Arriving a week before the female, the male claims his section of the hayfield or pasture and when she comes, does his utmost in song and deed to convince her he's the one of her dreams – the bird she flew all the way from Argentina to meet. True birds of open spaces, bobolinks sing on the wing – a loud bubbling, cheerful song unlike any other bird in our grasslands.

Bobolinks are late nesters, at least when compared to the red-winged blackbirds, whose young may have already fledged by the first week in June. Bobolinks dilly and sing and dally and sing and don't get down to serious homemaking until late May. If their nests are in hayfields many are destroyed by the first cutting of hay. Likewise in grazed paddocks. Forty cows, or 160 hoofs, on half an acre for twelve hours a day have a tendency to smash a lot of nests and eggs.

Aldo Leopold wrote in his landmark paper "A Biotic View of Land" that "... a good farm must be one where the wild fauna and flora has lost acreage without losing its existence." What has worked well on our farm is to lightly graze one field when the grass reaches six to eight inches of growth, usually around the middle of May, and then let it go for hay. This allows the grassland birds, especially the bobolinks and vesper sparrows, time for nest building, egg laying, and raising their families before the field is cut. Some years, depending upon the weather and the amount of hay needed, we'll wait an extra week or ten days to cut and then use the hay for heifers and dry cows or horses. Our goal is to see flying young bobolinks while we're mowing the field. Reward enough for a bit more mature forage. In good bobolink years, we have counted up to forty-five singing males in one twelve-acre field.

Other benefactors of delayed hay cutting are the ring-necked pheasants, bobwhite quail, and cottontail rabbits. The pheasants and quail are mostly gone from our county. The bobwhite never fully recovered following the severe winters of the 1970s. Two years ago a covey was raised on the farm and spent a lot of time in the potato patch eating beetles. But the cottontails are doing fine, in part on account of the West Nile Virus outbreak in 2002 that greatly reduced the local population of great horned owls, their number one predator. Since then the cottontails have reproduced, well, like rabbits.

I can walk through the orchard at any time and see six or eight cottontails sitting motionless in their daytime "beds" in the blackberry patch. For several winters I have considered "collecting" a cottontail for fried rabbit and candied yams, but I haven't found the heart to do it. I practically know them by name as they make their early evening visits to the crib for corn-on-the-cob.

The cottontails around the farm buildings are also protected from the pair of red foxes that is raising a litter of pups in a woodchuck burrow in the east fencerow. The fox dine on young hayfield red-winged blackbirds instead of cottontails.

I have often wondered how the female cottontail rabbit excavates her nesting hollow—half the size of a football—without leaving any soil around the edges. Does she dig with such energy that the soil is so spread out that it's undetectable? Probably. It is surely done to avoid detection by predators such as the opossum and red fox. She then plucks fur from her breast and fills the nest before the young are born. When the muzzle of a grazing cow approaches the nest the young cottontails will squirm and jerk beneath their furry cover giving the appearance of some weird legless animal. The cow will likely sidestep the odd creature and graze elsewhere and the baby rabbits will live for another day.

All this takes place in May, a wonderful month once it comes. May's full moon is sometimes called the Flower Moon. This year [*2007, ed.*], May has two, one on the second and the other on the thirty-first. I make a motion to name the second full moon the Grass Moon.

Summer

On May 28, I saw the first monarch butterfly of the year. I was raking hay when the butterfly appeared, checking the clover blossoms for nectar. I have seen more since.

I always wonder which generation of monarchs it is, from those that migrated south through here last October to overwinter in sanctuaries in the Mexican state of Michoacán.

The monarchs leave their winter home in Mexico usually in late February through mid-March and it is thought they may fly as far north as Texas and Oklahoma before succumbing to old age.

The monarchs arriving here in late spring are likely the second or third generation of last year's last hatch. The first ones to hatch here in late spring and early summer may then fly on north into Canada and into New England. This generation will live only two months. It is our last hatch of the summer that lives the long life and flies the long journey to Mexico. These migrants enter into a non-productive phase known as diapause and may live up to eight months or more. Once they begin their return journey, diapause ends and the monarchs mate and start depositing eggs on milkweeds, and future generations are assured.

The monarchs provide the visual change that carries spring into summer, while the call of the gray tree frog provides the audible proof. During these warm and rainy nights, the tree frogs call incessantly. It is such a nice sound to drift off to sleep to ... rain and frog music ... the promise of the abundance of summer.

Unlike many parts of the nation, our rains have been gentle and timely; no hard soil-caking downpours and no extended dry spells. First cutting hay is a vast improvement over a year ago and so are the pastures. Corn is up and growing and the oats are nice. Farming with all its weather and market uncertainties must be the most interesting work on earth. In spite of the hazards, the farmers are jovial.

What really adds to their joy is the likely possibility of a dramatic boost of the price of milk at the farm gate for the second half of the year. With milk now at $18.00 CWT., some see at least a $6.00 to $8.00 CWT. increase by late summer and through the fall and winter. There are a number of reasons for this: one is the price of overseas milk. New Zealand will likely see $27.00 CWT. milk and Canada around $30.00. Of course, those prices are in U.S. dollars. And with the dollar weak in relationship to foreign currencies, dairy imports are not an attractive option for the processors. The flipside is that the weak greenback encourages exports.

Second, with grain prices at record highs, large dairies may be tempted to cut back on grain feeding, which will reduce milk production, further pressuring an upward price trend. Some dairy economists say the large confined dairies purchasing all their feed will need $30.00 CWT. milk in order to break even. Especially if corn hits $7.00 a bushel as many predict. From all appearances, the playing field is far from level at this stage of the game and definitely favors the dairies that produce most or all of their own feed.

Quality forages are another unknown, with some hay growing regions hard hit by rains, making it difficult to harvest hay when it is at its top value. Good first cutting hay is already selling for $150.00 a ton west of the Mississippi. We are having our problems here with good hay drying conditions lasting only a day or two before heat, humidity, and rain move in. A lot of baleage is being made to preserve the quality of the hay.

The rains which hinder the haymaking suit the gray tree frogs just fine. They call with gusto and last night a barn owl joined the chorus … a trill here and a shriek there.

(2008)

140

Red-tailed Hawks

In late September, a pair of red-tailed hawks started building a nest seventy feet up in a black walnut tree in the middle of our lower pasture field. The pair worked at a leisurely pace through the golden days of autumn, a stick here and a twig there, and the nest began to take shape. By mid-November it was completed.

The hawks must be an experienced older pair, because the nest is well and securely placed in a four-pronged fork, and it survived the early November storm that ravaged Wooster and flattened local corn fields. It was built for the long haul. From my vantage point the nest appears to be of a size that would fill a wheelbarrow with sticks.

Measuring at least three feet in diameter at breast height, the black walnut towers to ninety feet or more, and lumbermen have gazed upon it with desire for its value as veneer timber. Since the tree is in the open, it is branchy. I could never see much sense in sacrificing a massive tree for a ten-foot saw log. Neither could my dad. So we left it in peace and harvested its annual crop of walnuts.

The tree always yields more walnuts than we use, and those are harvested by the fox squirrels. All winter, squirrel tracks cross the 150 feet of meadow to the tree and then back to the woods like spokes leading from the hub of a wheel. Around the base of the tree, cracked walnuts litter the ground like gravel. I understand the squirrels' fondness for the nuts because the meats are big and plump and exceptionally sweet.

When the hawks began work on the nest, I thought it a bit odd for redtails to be building a nest in the autumn, so I checked the literature.

Bruce Peterjohn in his *Birds of Ohio* said that Lou Campbell reported a pair beginning nest construction as early as January

141

24th. John K. Terres in *Encyclopedia of North American Birds* likewise says as early as January. Arthur Cleveland Bent in his *Life Histories of North American Birds* doesn't give an early nest building date, but he does say that red-tailed hawks "stake out their claim" late in February, a month before the eggs are laid. He was likely referring to New England, where spring is short and late, or absent. Frank and John Craighead, in *Hawks, Owls and Wildlife*—a report on their thorough study of raptors in southern Michigan—say mid-February.

In spite of what the experts said, our redtails did build in the fall when the weather was a lot more pleasant for homebuilding than it would have been in January. Plus interest rates were low. All of the experts also write that red-tailed hawks are cautious during nest construction and will stay away from the site if humans are nearby. This pair was not shy at all. Our family camped one evening and into the next forenoon about three hundred feet downstream from the nest, and the hawks went on with their nest-building while we watched.

Now that the nest is finished, the pair is patiently waiting for March to lay their two eggs. Early the other morning, both were soaring over the farm and one screamed its shrill cry, which has been described as similar to the squeal of a pig or steam escaping from a teapot. To me it simply sounded like the familiar and wild call of the redtail.

The red-tailed hawks are common in the neighborhood and have nested on our farm before, but it was always in the woods and in oak trees that tenaciously cling to their heavy leaves until late fall. We were hardly aware they had nested until we heard the hesitant calls of the young in late summer. Here in the walnut tree they will be much more visible because walnuts leaf out late in the spring and then drop their leaves early in the fall. Besides, from the ridge in our woods, the redtails' nest will almost be at eye level and should give us a good view during incubation, feeding, and rearing of their young.

Locally, redtails are still called "chicken hawks" for their supposed preference for domestic fowl. Friends who have laying hens in an "egg mobile," tell me that redtails do take an occasional "free-range" chicken. Smart hawks. According to the Craigheads' study in Michigan, sixty percent of the red-tailed hawk's prey is the meadow mouse or vole. The rest ranges from cottontail rabbits to snakes.

The talons of a redtail are formidable objects, as I discovered one autumn. We have a V-top house sparrow trap that supplies needed protein for our barn cats, to supplement their milk diet. There were a few house sparrows in the trap, which attracted a migrating Cooper's hawk. It pushed its way through the narrow V of wire and ate the cats' sparrows, but then was also trapped.

A hunting redtail saw the Cooper's hawk and forced, I still can't understand how, its big body through the V-top meant for house sparrows. Once the redtail was inside, it realized its mistake and dropped the idea of eating its cousin. Now it too was trapped. When I approached, the hawks were waiting at opposite ends of the trap. I caught the fierce-eyed Cooper's hawk, which turned quite passive, and released it.

The redtail was a different bird. It flipped over on its back and presented its sharp and powerful talons. I gingerly offered my foot and sacrificed a new Tingley boot. So I pulled on my gloves and picked up the irritated hawk. It righted itself, gripped my arm with its free leg and sank its talons through the lined chore coat, flannel shirt, and deep into my wrist as easily as penetrating Swiss cheese. I endured the pain and carried the hawk, like a falconer, to the house for the family to see. Then I released my grip and after a few moments, the hawk relaxed its hold on me and flew away. It felt good.

Fall

It seems almost sinful when a dry period in late summer has one glancing with an expectant eye for a hurricane to bring needed rain. Hurricane Fay brought us two days of drizzle and about half-an-inch of total moisture. It helped. Gustaf ran like a spooked horse north into Canada just to the west of us and left us with only a sprinkle.

But now Ike is battering Cuba and may eventually track north and east. Who knows what will happen along the Gulf Coast. As farmers, we patiently wait on the early rains and the late rains and have the confidence that it will all work out for the good of all.

Autumn is a fine time of the year. The nesting season is over and the birds are in that pause before winter. Some migrants are arriving. A winter wren is right outside in the lilac bush. Last evening, common nighthawks on their way south for the cold months, were seining the air for insects. Turkey vultures, too, are loafing their way south.

The other morning we butchered some of our broilers. After everything was over and the wheelbarrow loaded with what remained, I wheeled it far back to the field where a young red-tailed hawk spends most of the days patiently watching for mice. In other words, I brought the young hawk breakfast.

Later in the day I went back to the fields and the redtail had company. Close to twenty turkey vultures were in a semicircle by the hawk's broiler buffet. I watched from a quarter-mile away and pondered how one would describe the flock of ponderous vultures dining on chicken, and concluded they simply looked like a bunch of buzzards.

The redtail obviously had eaten its fill. I have noticed whenever redtails and vultures compete for food, the red-tailed hawk is dominant. They eat first and the vultures get what is left. Have we ever considered what the countryside would be like without carrion-eaters such as the turkey vultures? My brother had a cow that died and since she was in an area far from the road, they left her for the vultures. We agreed that the knacker man is getting to be expensive. He counted thirty vultures soaring above the dead cow at one time. In a couple of days the job was finished.

On to something less morbid. The bees are doing well, although not nearly as much honey has been made as last year. So far, the farming year has been good in spite of almost no rain in August. We have enough hay for the winter, nice oats, and enough corn. Grain commodity prices don't affect us here very much. I think Fred Kirschenman had a point when he said that we should produce nothing that is traded on the Chicago Board of Trade.

As far as the overall economy, one hears various opinions. The wheels came off Freddie Mac and Fannie Mae, the mortgage giants, and they are both now on life support. One of our former agricultural extension agents once said of this county of many small-scale farms and businesses, "We may never hit the highs of the economy, but we also never hit the lows."

I did hear several sawmill operators talking and they mentioned one item that is in strong demand in their lumber business: railroad ties. Any tree, outside of the softwoods such as linden and aspen, can be sawn into seven-inch by nine-inch by eight-foot six-inches long and sold for ties. One of them saws some twenty-four-footers for switching track ties. Someone even said that Warren Buffet took money out of China oil and invested it in U.S. railroads. Amtrak is running every coach available. Interesting.

May your autumn be blessed with a long Indian summer, and your Thanksgiving Day, with love and family.

(2008)

Winter

In seed-time learn, in harvest teach, in winter enjoy.
—William Blake (1757–1827)

We had our first snow of the season last night. An inch of the white stuff was driven by a fierce west/northwest wind that cut to the marrow in spite of multiple layers of flannel. It is one of those days when outdoor work is cut to a minimum and more attention is given to the hearth fire.

At this writing, most of the wood furnishing our heat is from a buckeye tree. The tree had been girdled by a herd of bored goats and had died over a span of several years. Since the three-foot-across buckeye was leaning precariously over our daughter and son-in-law's springhouse, it was decided that the big tree had to go.

So a woodcutting day was planned to fill our front porch. But how could we take down the buckeye without flattening the springhouse and without hiring a professional tree removal crew? After surveying the situation, we pooled our tree-cutting expertise, which didn't take long, and decided to tie a rope as far up in the tree as the nimblest of us could climb and then put tension on the rope with a tractor.

With much advice from the sidelines, the sawyer worked on the trunk, which turned out to be hollow to within four inches of the outer bark. The saw cut through the last inches and the buckeye broke free, and pulled by the rope, crashed down precisely where we wanted it to fall. I was surprised at how easily it could be persuaded to fall opposite to its natural inclination toward the springhouse.

Once we started cutting the buckeye into firewood, I could understand why it was easy to pull. It is the lightest wood I've ever worked with in all my years of firewood cutting. Since we are on the northern fringe of the buckeye's range, the tree was new to me as a source of firewood. Buckeye makes linden and pine seem like hardwood. Besides, the light and rough-barked wood doesn't burn well. It burns, but not well by itself. Left to itself in the woodstove it will die overnight. When mixed with oak, ash, red elm, and other choice firewood, the buckeye works fine.

Soon after our day of cutting buckeye, I read where Abraham Lincoln flew into a rare fury when it was suggested that he acquiesce to the South and allow new states entering the Union to become slave states. "I would go to Washington without the countenance of the men that supported me and were my friends before the election; I would be as powerless as a block of *buckeye* wood."

Now knowing what President Lincoln said, I can't understand the logic behind naming our state after a tree that is powerless and bears an inedible nut. I'm also aware that one should never sniff a gift fish, so I'm very grateful for our porch stacked full of seasoned firewood.

Possibly more now than anytime since the 1930s, practical skills of living from the land, such as firewood cutting, are needed. Bill Henning writes on a model for sustainability in farming. As Bill suggests, with the downturn in housing and sawmilling and the resulting scarcity in shavings and sawdust for livestock bedding, farmers may need to consider growing their bedding in the form of straw or corn fodder.

A number of garden seed companies reported almost a hundred percent increase in sales for 2008. As a result, some farmer's markets had lower sales for the year. Where the economy will go is anyone's guess. Some envision a short period of deflation followed by hyperinflation. One positive out of all this uncertainty is the lower fuel prices for homes not set up for woodburners. It will help to warm the winter.

May your homes and hearts be filled with warmth and cheer during the holiday and winter seasons.

(2008)

Spring

Smoke and steam are roiling from sugar camps around the community and fresh maple syrup is on the menu; on pancakes, French toast, and fried corn mush. If you are a part of the gathering and boiling down of the sap to syrup, you know that it simply tastes better than any you can buy.

We had a three-day run and then the jet stream looped south again, opening our back door to frigid Canadian air that then promptly shut down our small enterprise. But good weather is forecast for later in the week—nighttime twenties and daytimes sunny and high thirties. Weather that will heave the farmer's alfalfa roots out of the ground is ideal for the maple syrup man.

According to most local folks our winter has been a long and cold one. Where the ground was snow-covered, it never froze to a great depth. Underneath driveways and other places where the snow was removed, water pipes were frozen. In the hard winter of 1976–77 all our water pipes froze, except from the cistern to the cattle watering trough, our most crucial water line. That stayed open because there was a slow leak at its lower end in the piggery. All our house water was supplied by the hand pump on our hand-dug well in the yard. Of course, our children were small and didn't demand a daily tub bath and we survived the winter in fine shape. Eventually the weather warmed, spring arrived on schedule, and when the pipes thawed out in late March there was cause for celebration. I hope that is an indicator for the economy.

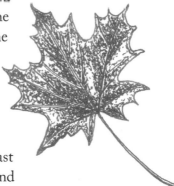

What a difference a year makes. Last spring we worried about high grain and fuel costs and there were predictions of milk prices hitting record highs by autumn. Somewhere along the way things went awry, New York banks toppled like dominos, the economy changed directions, and so did the grand economic projections. Once the housing bubble ruptured and sank like a lead balloon, it brought practically every commodity down with its demise. Crude oil is at a third of its high point, grain prices are down, ethanol plants would be doomed were it not for hefty government subsidies, milk and cattle prices are down, and nobody seems to know where it will end.

Nassim Taleb, author of the *The Black Swan*, a book on economics, writes that asking an economist to predict the future is like asking the Christmas turkey what's for dinner on Christmas. Based on its entire lifetime of experience, the turkey expects to be fed on Christmas, not to be eaten.

My parents married in January 1929 and started farming that spring. As Dad would say, "Just as things started rolling ... the wrong direction." In October the stock market crashed. Andrew Mellon, Secretary of the Treasury, said, "The fundamentals of the economy are sound." *Variety*, the show business paper was closer to the truth as it reported, "Wall Street lays an egg."

Although Henry Ford had declared in the late 1920s that, "Machinery is the new Messiah," as a new car or new Fordson tractor rolled off his assembly line every ten seconds, the agricultural depression deepened. Ford's tractors did to the Great Plains what "no hailstorm, no blizzard, no tornado, no drought, no epic siege of frost, no prairie fire, nothing in the natural history of the southern plains had ever done. They removed the native prairie grass ... so completely that by the end of 1931 it was a different land – thirty-three million acres stripped bare in the southern plains." [from *The Worst Hard Times*, Timothy Egan]

The stage was set for the Dust Bowl and the Dirty Thirties when millions of tons of topsoil blew away. Ships at sea, three hundred miles off the Atlantic coast, were covered with brown dirt from the dust storms. Photographs showing farm foreclosure sales in Iowa, Kansas, and Oklahoma are not nice. John Steinbeck's *Grapes of Wrath* tells part of the story of getting out and moving west. Timothy Egan's more recent book, *The Worst Hard Time*, tells the story of those who stayed.

In spite of the collapse, my parents lived well in those tough times because they ate well on home-grown fruits, vegetables, grains, eggs, milk, and meat. The only thing that was scarce, Dad said, was money. All their remaining years, influenced by the decade of the 30s, they nurtured and practiced typical Midwestern caution and frugality, and passed the belief on to us that the very best food one can possess is grown on your own land.

(2009)

Eating Well at Home

In the summer of 2007, our daughter and son-in-law were offered Victorian trim from the porch of an old farmhouse that was to be torn down following damage from a tornado. They had been on the lookout for something to spiff up their house's porch and jumped at the opportunity and immediately began rounding up "volunteers" for the project.

The damaged house was near Loudonville and Fred Cannon was project director. The rest of us were designated as lifters and carriers to get the trim (some may call it gingerbread; I call it hard-to-paint) loaded on Fred's trailer and strapped down for the twenty-mile trip to David and Emily's farm.

While the rest of the crew relaxed around the picnic lunch of cheese and crackers and apple pie spread out on the grass beneath one of the yard's sugar maples, I wandered through the house checking for treasures, since the owner had said anything can go. Some books were strewn across the floor of the living room. Picking up one of the older ones that was slightly water-damaged from the storm, I discovered it was a *1921 Agricultural Yearbook*.

Every year, the United States Department of Agriculture publishes a yearbook, and I must confess that out of the dozen or so I have, most are tedious to read. This one, however, is a gem. The introduction is Secretary of Agriculture Henry C. Wallace's report to President Woodrow Wilson. American agriculture, flourishing on the heels of World War I, (wheat peaked at three dollars a bushel in 1919), had suddenly tanked toward the end of 1920. Secretary Wallace reported to the President that "… there were no shortcuts by which an immediate return to agricultural prosperity could be insured." Now in its infancy in 1921, the agricultural depression was well along before the hard times hit

Main Street in 1929 – the decade in which the invisible hand of Adam Smith became the bloody claw of survival.

Gloomy forecast aside, what is fascinating about the *Yearbook* is the many maps spread throughout its 884 pages. Corn, for instance, shows an average yearly yield of 2.8 billion bushels for the eight years prior to 1921. Of that total, forty percent was fed to hogs on the farms where it was grown, which is understandable, but 3.5 percent was used as human food on the farms … cornmeal in cornbread, pone, and fried mush soaked with gravy or maple syrup. Hominy and grits in the South.

Two maps that are especially revealing show vegetables grown on farms for home use only and vegetables grown for sale. The map for home use only is almost black with dots from about the one-hundredth meridian east to the Atlantic; the region covered by Peterson's *Guide to the Birds of Eastern and Central North America*. Each dot is the size of the period at the end of this sentence and represents a value of $25,000 of vegetables in 1919. The largest gardens were in Virginia and Massachusetts, about one-half acre, and the smallest in the prairie and plains states, about one-fifth acre.

The second map shows the acreage of vegetables grown for sale, excluding white and sweet potatoes. Each dot represents five-hundred acres and outside of a band of land south of Lake Ontario from Buffalo to Utica, New York; from Long Island to Norfolk, Virginia, and the Imperial Valley in California, the map is almost empty of dots. Farm families were growing their own food and were fairly well prepared for the coming lean times of the Depression.

My choice garden on the farm is our kitchen garden. I pass it every day on the way to the barn and fields. The garden has a nice blend of domestic and wild. There are flowers and plants for butterflies, bees, and hummingbirds; early lettuce, red potatoes, radishes, Siberian tomatoes, and sugar snap peas, if they survive the grandchildren, for us. Within minutes after leaving the garden, the vegetables can be on the table in chicken or beef stir-fries and salads, and eating doesn't get any better, taste and health wise.

That first meal of red skin potatoes, fresh from the garden, spread with melting butter and then covered with fresh cucumber salad has to rank near the top of foods known to humankind. One of my mother's and my favorite summertime meals was simply new potatoes boiled-in-the-skin, which were mashed in cereal bowls with an old wooden handled fork, liberally spread with butter, seasoned with salt and black pepper, and then covered with Guernsey milk. I would watch the butter and pepper float to the top of the milk and swirl in little eddies before dipping my spoon in and partaking of the hot potatoes and cold milk. Oh, by the way, my mother lived to be ninety-one and was never in a hospital until the last two nights of her life.

My wife is the serious gardener here. I do prepare the gardens for her. The kitchen garden I spade or till, and the big garden, or patch, I cover generously with strawy barn manure and then plow with Davey and Kenny and an old Oliver 404 two-horse walking plow. It is sort of a rite of spring—peepers are piping and I am plowing. The silt-loam soil crumbles so nicely that I finish fitting it with the spike-toothed harrow and then she plants, usually with the help of several grandchildren.

Although my wife spends many wintertime hours poring over seed catalogs and gets her orders in early, she also saves many seeds such as Ladyfinger popcorn, Siberian tomato, winter lettuce, Jacob's cattle and numerous other colorful and interesting kinds of beans, as well as Reid's yellow dent field corn (for cornmeal). Tomatoes and many other plants are started indoors and by late March every windowsill facing to the south and east is filled with trays sprouting our summer's bounty.

The frost-sensitive plants aren't set out until the soil has warmed and frost no longer threatens. Our main crop of potatoes, Yukon Gold, is planted in one of the cornfields around the May full moon, unless the full moon is too early in the month and our field corn hasn't been planted yet. It is a family project and all our children and grandchildren living near us share the work and potatoes and the camaraderie.

The Yukon Gold is a short season plant and is harvested before the corn is ready. It doesn't yield as much as the white Kennebec, but once you've seen and tasted Yukon Gold mashed potatoes, there is no going back.

The sweet corn, likewise, is planted in a field with the regular corn. There is not enough space in the gardens to supply the corn for our family. Like the potatoes, the entire family shares the bounty of the succulent maize from the home farm. The sweet corn is planted along the outside of the field and its growing season is finished by silo filling time and thus the field is open and ready to go for the silage cutters. Having the sweet corn along the edge also makes it easier for the raccoons to find. Our family prefers the Incredible variety of sweet corn and so do the 'coons. Even with the destructive habits of the masked bandits, there is always enough corn for everyone.

So it is with all the gardens and vegetables ... enough for everyone. The present grim economic conditions should be no reason for those of us fortunate enough to be living on good land not to be eating well and sharing it with others less privileged.

Summer

As Bromfield wrote in the preface to *Out of the Earth*, "All of us love the fields and the cattle. Most of us are simple people who love what we are doing, and that is perhaps the greatest satisfaction in life one can have." A recent study (I tend to be leery of statistics) claimed that eighty percent of the American people don't like their job. That is hard to imagine.

When I am cultivating corn on a seventy-five-degree late June day with a team that responds perfectly to my voice, and I listen to the cheerful flight songs of the bobolinks in the hayfield nearby, I think we farmers must be the most fortunate people on earth; in loving the independence and modesty of our work, in living a life close to the soil. A way of living as well as a way of thinking. As Terry Tempest Williams said, "Living on a place instead of merely residing there."

To speak of bobolinks ... for years we have agonized over waiting to cut hay until the bobolinks have finished nesting. Especially if a week of perfect hay-drying weather showed up in late spring.

Flying north from their winter home in Argentina, the male bobolinks arrive on our farm the last week in April and the females a week or two later. Instead of then settling down and setting up housekeeping like the redwings and savannah sparrows do, bobolinks wait until late May or early June to nest. Thus most of their nests are destroyed when the hay is cut. This year our son-in-law, who enjoys the birds as much as I do, suggested we lightly graze the twelve-acre field early and then wait to cut for hay until late June. How clever.

The bobolinks love it. Observing the field, I can't help but notice how much the grasses (orchard and timothy) emulate the native prairie that was the bobolinks' original habitat. Big bluestem, the predominant grass of the tall grass prairie, is a warm season grass that emerges slowly in the spring. We have two clumps of big bluestem by the mailbox and the grass is only about a foot tall as I write this. Almost exactly the height of the grasses in the lightly-grazed hayfield. It finally dawned on me that the reason the bobolinks fiddle around before nesting is to give the warm season grasses time to grow and provide cover.

The red-winged blackbirds, on the other hand, are native to wetlands and cattail marshes and have to nest early before they get smothered in the lush growth of the tall swamp forbs. In our hayfields, the redwings tend to weave their nests off the ground in the woody stems of dock and fleabane, while bobolinks nest on the ground. Bobolink nests are hard to find, because, like many prairie-nesting birds, the female runs away from its nest before flying. An excellent way of nest-hiding.

Every June, our family walks the oat fields to pull mustard (locally called wild radishes) and dock to prevent them from going to seed. The old saying that "one year's seed is seven years' weeds" is certainly true for members of the mustard family. Closer to the truth for "wild radishes" is that one year of going to seed means the pest weed will be on the farm forever. Remember the saying from the gospels of Matthew and Luke, "faith like a mustard seed" – they are small ... and abundant. This year the evening was humid, and before we finished, the gray tree frogs began calling.

The first dark of evening is now announced by the calls of these little tree-climbing frogs. Their oft-repeated, woodpecker-like trill is a sound strong enough to carry spring into summer, and as we farmers and gardeners wait for rain, it carries with it a hint of a thundershower sometime after midnight.

Tree frogs don't begin their chorus until the rush of spring is over and the bud has turned to leaf, and the seed has been planted and sprouted, and we know that it's now a matter of soil and sun and rain. The tree frogs' call is the last sound I hear before drifting off to sleep ... and we wait for rain.

(2009)

Bats

We had just brought the cows into the milking stable one evening, when suddenly a birdlike creature took flight and silently zigzagged around posts and partitions. One of the girls screamed, "A bat!" Several cats quickly scrambled up onto stanchions, hoping to snatch the flying morsel. In the excitement, someone stepped on the tomcat, and his yowl added to the din. The bat, bewildered by the lantern light and the commotion, finally alighted on an overhead joist and scurried into a crack where two beams overlapped. Peace and tranquility returned to the stable.

Bats have the worst image of any creature in the natural world, with the possible exception of the snake. This is especially true in Western society. Bats are considered to be dirty, to be carriers of rabies, to live in dark, dank attics and caves, to get tangled in one's hair. Then too, bats are often associated with wickedness. The Evil One is often depicted with the wings of a bat.

Bats also figure prominently in folklore, superstition, and sorcery. For the Chinese, they have long been symbols of happiness. In Austria there was a belief that if one carried the left eye of a bat on his person, he would be invisible. And ancient medical concoctions often contained parts of bats: an ointment made of "frankincense, lizards' blood, and bats' blood in equal parts" was used to cure trachoma, an eye disease. Likewise, a blend of "bats' heads pounded and mixed with honey" was a remedy for poor eyesight.

If one has abnormal things aflutter in the cranium, he is said to be "batty" or else to have "bats in the belfry."

But despite the bad things said about bats, and regardless of whether we like them or not, they are fascinating and useful creatures. And they are the only mammals that can fly. (Flying squirrels are gliders, not true flyers.) The Papago Indians in the

Southwest use guano (droppings) from desert bats, gathered from churches and mountain caves, to fertilize their fields.

Many misconceptions surround our perception of bats. For one, they are not blind. They have eyes and can see in varying degrees. What they lack in sight is made up for by their keen hearing. Studies done in Sweden on captive animals showed that a bat can hear a fly cleaning its wings or rubbing its legs together. The bat would then dart in that direction and snap up the fly.

Scientists call the bat's amazing ability to use echoes of its own voice to locate food and obstacles, echolocation. The bat accomplishes this by emitting intensely loud high-frequency bursts of sound and then interpreting the echoes. In this way the bat can judge the distance, direction, and movement of insect prey, and the nature of nearby objects that reflect sound. Thus, if you hang a string across an opening of a building where bats leave and enter, they will never fly into the string.

Bats are widely distributed throughout the temperate and tropical regions of the world. Around nine hundred species are recognized, by far the greatest number of which live in the tropics.

Many of the tropical bats feed on fruit, pollen, and nectar. These bats hunt by sight and smell instead of sonar.

The vampire bats of Central and South America feed at night on the blood of living animals. Vampires use echolocation to find their prey. Landing near the sleeping victim, they crawl aboard and use their razor-sharp incisor teeth to make a quick gash in the skin. Their saliva contains an anticoagulant to keep the blood from clotting. Once the incision is made, the vampire drinks its fill and then flies away.

The bats found in the United States and Canada don't eat fruit or drink blood. They feed only on insects. Bats drink water as purple martins do. Skimming over the water, they scoop up a drink with their lower jaw.

The bat seen by most of us on warm summer evenings, darting

this way then that way, snatching flying insects, is the little brown bat. Weighing but a quarter of an ounce, it is common around farm buildings and villages where it finds hideaways in cracks in beams, enclosed cornices, and attics. In late spring the female gives birth to a single offspring, rarely to twins. The young grow rapidly and are able to fly when about three weeks old. When they are a month old they leave the home shelter and start hunting on their own.

Banding studies suggest that sometime in late September many of the little brown bats leave their summer haunts and congregate in caves by the thousands where, insulated from the cold, they will hibernate through the winter. Most of the bats in Ohio and Indiana are thought to overwinter in Kentucky caves, although five caves near Akron, Ohio, are used by thousands of hibernating little brown bats every winter.

In 2006, in one of these overwintering caves near Albany, New York, a deadly disease was discovered in hibernating bats. A mysterious fungus, scientists called it "white-nose syndrome" (WNS) from the white powdery substance on the bats' heads and wings and especially around their noses. Nearly 11,000 bats were killed by the fungus in the Albany cave.

Within two years the disease had spread to large parts of New England and now new outbreaks have been found in Pennsylvania, Virginia, and West Virginia. In some hibernating caves, bat mortality has been over ninety percent and an estimated one million wintering bats have died from WNS.

Scientists studying the disease are fairly certain that the fungus is transmitted from bat to bat, which can cluster in bunches of three-hundred bats per square foot. Scientists also believe that humans may inadvertently carry the fungus from cave to cave. For that reason many caves have now been closed to public access during the bat hibernation months in an effort to slow the rapidly spreading disease.

Many of the stricken bats are emaciated and lack body fat and show erratic behavior. One has to wonder whether there is a connection to colony collapse disorder (CCD) that has devastated the honeybees this past decade. The bees show similar behavior in becoming disoriented and dying away from the hive.

So far no cases of WNS have been found west of Pennsylvania. While Ohio is home to thirteen species of bats, the little brown is the most common. Our neighbors to the north harbor hundreds of little brown bats in their barn and I hope the little mammals overwinter there in the hollow dry old beams and are protected from the devastating fungus. What would the late spring and summer evenings be like without the little bats seining the warm air for insects?

Fall

For some odd reason I enjoy watching turkey vultures, especially here around the autumnal equinox. The big birds loaf their way south by the hundreds from summer homes north of us. Soaring and catching rising thermals in the pristine September sky, they circle for what seems like hours without any great effort on their part. But all the while the vultures are on the lookout for a free lunch.

A couple of days ago I saw a dozen or so vultures assembled in our neighbor's pasture field. I don't know what set them off, likely a place at the table, but two of them got into a serious squabble. The buzzards would run at each other and pummel with their big wings. Then they would back off, rest, and go at it again. Throughout the clash, the rest of the gang stood back and watched with what appeared to be only mild interest. After four or five rounds, the one had had enough and took wing for friendlier eateries.

In all my years of farming and observing the natural world, I had never seen turkey vultures get into a brawl. I always thought that in the bird kingdom, buzzards get along with each other very amiably in sharing road kills, afterbirth, dead possums, skunks, and woodchucks. Now I know that the solemn birds have a line that too can be crossed.

As Rachel Carson noted, there is "a sense of wonder" connected to nature. Often, we are surprised by the unexpected. I had another such occurrence in early summer. My friend and neighbor let me know that there was a swarm of honeybees clustered on a fencepost along their oats field. Actually, there were two swarms and they were clearly what we beekeepers call "after-swarms."

In such cases the main or prime swarm, along with the old queen, leaves the colony, and for reasons not fully understood, the colony keeps spinning off small swarms. Most of them are too weak in numbers to build up into a strong colony and store up enough honey to survive the winter. I combined ours with a split Sam had made for us. I couldn't find either queen and decided that "may the best woman win" and Sam's queen won out. (Sam's young queen was a well-bred Italian and her offspring were nice yellow bees; the swarm bees were darker.)

Leroy has told me since that the bee tree produced two more small swarms that his nephew hived. Obviously, the colony was super strong to produce five swarms and still thrive as they are doing in the black walnut tree. This is the intriguing part—Leroy and I have noted that the only wild bees we are aware of are in black walnut trees. Our son has had a colony in a black walnut tree by the end of their driveway for seven years now. They are doing fine.

Why in this age of high varroa and tracheal mites infestations are these wild bee colonies doing so well? There must be something in the wood of live black walnut that controls the mites. We farmers know that walnut sawdust, if used as bedding, can harm horses' feet and cause mastitis in dairy cows. Could it kill mites without harming the honeybee? As an experiment, our son got some fresh black walnut sawdust from his friend's mill and I spread it on the pull-out tray beneath the screened bottom board. I change it once a month.

The State bee inspector found no mites in our "walnut tree" colony. Our older hive, where I had just started the walnut treatment a week before his visit, did have varroa mites. By late October I want him to check again. Perhaps we are on to an easy and simple method to control the mites that cause millions of dollars of losses to America's beekeepers.

In this part of the country we are nearing the end of an excellent year. We had enough of a drought in July to stunt the grasses into dormancy and then with the seven inches of soaking rains in August, pastures and hay fields exploded. We are putting up our last hay for the season and it should carry us into April. I am of the Bio-dynamic/Rudolph Steiner philosophy that the best feed for your animals is grown at home.

The best of autumns to all.

(2009)

Winter

It is December and the unmistakable signs of winter are beginning to seep in around the edges. While the dairy herd is still grazing fall-sown oats and turnips seeded in the corn following the last cultivation (an experiment in late June and a success), a few snow flurries fly, morning temperatures are in the upper 20s and low 30s, tundra swans are migrating southeast, and more winter birds are at the feeders, hinting that the cold season is around the corner.

Feeding birds is certainly one of the pleasures of winter. For as long I can remember, we have been a family of bird feeders. Back in the days when sunflower seeds were unavailable, or possibly unaffordable, my mother would have us gather black walnuts in early fall and run them through the hand-cranked corn sheller to remove the pulpy outer covering. Following that messy job, we would wash the walnuts and place them on a flat roof to dry and cure in the autumn sun.

Once the walnuts were properly dried, they were stored inside the farm shop in wire egg baskets where they remained fresh indefinitely. About twice a week, my assignment was to crack a pie pan full of walnuts for the birds. I didn't pick the meats out of the shells, except for the ones I ate myself, which were many. The nuthatches, titmice, and chickadees did that work themselves. Fine beef suet was saved from the fall butchering and hung in onion bags for the downy, hairy, red-bellied, and occasional red-headed woodpeckers.

For the ground-feeding birds, we spread cracked corn, usually chicken mash or ground cow feed. This suited the mourning doves, tree and song sparrows, and dark-eyed ("slate-colored" back then) juncos just fine. In the 1950s, bird feeding was done on the cheap and was as enjoyable as it is today.

In 2006, the late Tom Ross brought us his 2½ gallon pickle jar sunflower feeder. He and his wife were moving to Colorado to live near their daughter, Susan, and thought the feeder would be more useful here in the East. The feeder is actually a self-feeder, as the pickle jar screws onto a cast aluminum base which then sets on top of a five-foot-high two-inch-across steel pipe.

An aluminum cone provides a roof, and that is attached with a bolt through the bottom of the jar. The feeder is well constructed. Tom and his family used it for over thirty years before we got it. I did manage to break the original jar when I cleaned it last summer, but I was able to find a replacement. Tom had told me in case the jar breaks to check flea markets as they are readily obtainable.

While our traditional feeder is twelve feet away from the house, next to a young Canadian hemlock that affords the feeder birds some protection from the Cooper's hawk's desire for a meal of mourning dove, Tom's sunflower feeder is right outside the kitchen window. Most of the visitors to the feeder are common winter birds such as titmice, cardinals, chickadees, house finches, and white-breasted nuthatches, but we do get the occasional surprises. Twice in November, on the sixth and briefly on the sixteenth, a yellow-throated warbler came to the pickle jar for black oil sunflowers. Last winter a red-breasted nuthatch was a regular visitor.

Instead of cracking black walnuts, we now feed mostly black oil sunflowers, which is a favorite food source for many feeder visitors.

We buy the sunflowers in fifty-pound bags. A good investment. A whole lot cheaper entertainment than vacationing in Florida. We still spread ground and cracked corn for the ground-feeders, and use beef suet for the woodpeckers. Other birds will also feed on the suet, especially the Carolina wrens.

Although the signs all point to winter and the end of autumn and the year's growing season, we are all grateful for food, shelter, good land, and friends. Henceforth it is indoor time for the farm animals and for us, and feeder time for the birds.

May peace be your gift at Christmas and your blessing all year through.

(2009)

Pileated Woodpecker

All of the local species of woodpeckers have visited our feeders except the pileated. Only once have I seen the big red-crested bird in our yard and that was more or less a flyover with a brief stop in the maple tree.

There is a pair of pileated woodpeckers in the nearby woods that raised a brood of young last spring. Pileateds are usually wary, almost as spooky as great blue herons, but the male of this pair is surprisingly trusting. I see him and hear his loud cackle almost every day.

Our son and his wife and children are visiting her parents in Kansas and I'm helping with their chores. If I walk through the woods on my way back to the farm, I usually see one of the pair. The other day I watched the male demolish a dead tree, searching for carpenter ants. Chips would fly for a while and then he would pause to feed on the exposed insects. After ten to fifteen minutes of frantic feeding, the woodpecker opened his big wings, cackled, and flew up through the woods.

The pileated woodpecker appears almost as large as a crow. One birder described it as, "The size of a crow with the sturdiness of a kingfisher." *The Sibley Guide to Birds* lists the pileated at ten ounces and the crow at one pound. A considerable difference in weight.

It is surprising for the size of the pileated woodpecker that it survived the glory days of market hunting, or rather that period (late 1800s through the early 1900s) when quality repeating shotguns became available while there were few laws protecting passerine birds. Its near-relative, the ivory-billed woodpecker, was gone by the 1950s.

By 1920, the pileated woodpecker, was gone from much of its former range, as mature woodlands had been cleared for farming. Then during the Depression Years, many farms in the East were abandoned for more fertile and level land to the west and northwest. These vacated hill farms soon reverted to woodlands. What benefited the white-tailed deer and wild turkey also helped the pileated woodpecker. As long as there was enough dead wood around to harbor ants, beetles, and grubs, the pileated woodpecker thrived and made a slow but steady comeback. Here in Ohio, the pileated woodpecker is fairly common to locally common in the eastern third of the state. Well over one hundred pileated woodpeckers have been counted in one day on the Millersburg Christmas Bird Count.

That is good news, because I like the impressive bird with his bright red crest and prominent black and white wing pattern; the cock-of-the-woods, as pioneer naturalists called him. I like to watch him fly through the trees to swoop up onto a dead snag, cock his head one way, then the other way, cackle a time or two, and then lay into the wood and make the chips and chunks of rotten wood fly for a meal of ants.

The pileated woodpecker is a bird that knows what he wants.

Spring

Today, March 2nd, I saw the first robin. I know one robin doesn't make a spring, and he's not in the dooryard yet, but at least having one in the neighborhood helps. Also, buckets are hanging on spiles in maple trees, another sure sign that spring is in the air.

I don't have to belabor the long and snowy winter, but I can't recall a more overcast and snow-filled February. The month seemed to last forever. As a rule, February is a cold but sunfilled month. Temperatures may drop to the low teens at night but by noon icicles are dripping, snow is melting, and rivulets of water are flowing down the ditches.

Not this year. There would be some snowmelt and then another storm would move in overnight, refilling the opened paths. Any illusions we had that spring is near, vanished. We sat by the fire reading and eating popcorn and listened to the rumble of the snowplow as Don worked most of the night so that the milk trucks could get through in the morning. Those guys deserve our thanks for their strenuous and yet skillful work in the midst of swirling and blowing snow. In spite of near zero visibility at times, Don missed our mailbox every time.

Generally, February winds tend to be calm. Depending on a wind pump for water all of our farming years, I have become a close observer of wind patterns. Sometimes in February there would be three consecutive days of calm, and then a weather front would approach, winds would rise, and water was pumped. The same patterns appear in August. Two years ago in August, there were twelve straight days of no wind. Since the two months are the same distance from the solstice (winter and summer) I wonder whether it has to do with the spin of the earth? Sort of the Midwestern version of the doldrums.

One of these days the sun will shine, the thermometer will reach fifty degrees Fahrenheit, and we will have Mud Season, that period we endure before full spring arrives. The massive snow piles and their slow melting rate promise a prolonged Mud Season, which will be graciously endured because of what follows – spring peepers, skunk cabbage, hepatica, plowing, pasture, animals on grass, dandelions, and robins in the yard.

No matter how many false starts March has, or how cruelly the month treats us, we just can't stop loving spring. Perhaps it is as Yogi Berra said about baseball, "Ninety-five percent is half mental."

Recently I read where a group, let's call them positive psychologists, began to study happy people rather than the mentally ill. These psychologists had doubts that the observations made about neurotics were applicable to the rest of us. What the positive psychologists learned was that, while getting a new phone, or a new car, or a new high-end home did give us a burst of pleasure, the pleasure did not last. If we wanted to continue to feel the same spike of happiness, we soon needed another fix – yet another phone, yet another car, more stuff. They called that mode of pleasure-seeking the "hedonic treadmill."

This is what got my attention – the happiest people, the shrinks discovered, did not live their lives on this perpetual treadmill. Rather, these folks had raised their baseline mood in ways that did not require repeated doses of new stuff. The people most satisfied with life, it turned out, had strong social connections, found meaning in their work, got to exercise what they considered to be their highest talents, and had a sense of some higher purpose.

The positive psychologists confirmed scientifically, in other words, what we simple-living folks have been advocating all along: a life lived with less emphasis on acquisition has the effect of leaving more time for richer, more meaningful, less resource-intensive life rewards, making people happier.

In 1862, Ralph Waldo Emerson wrote about his friend Henry Thoreau, "He chose to be rich by making his wants few, and supplying them himself." Most of us probably don't want to live like Thoreau did, but sad-eyed Henry knew how to simplify and not step onto the hedonic treadmill.

(2010)

Staking Your Dreams

I was unloading the last load of manure when the lark took flight. Although I wanted to clean the spreader yet before lunch, and was late already, I couldn't help but watch the show. The male horned lark left the ground to my left and swiftly gained altitude. Every hundred feet or so, he would circle and sing and then continue his ascent. Finally when the lark was barely visible, he alternately soared and flapped in a large circle, constantly singing a soft twittering song.

I strained to watch until my eyes watered. After maybe ten minutes of showing off his aerial and musical skills to his supposed-to-be-impressed mate somewhere nearby in the hayfield, the lark folded his wings and dropped like a plumb bob. Waiting until the last second before opening his wings and gliding to land almost at the very spot he took flight from, the lark really impressed me, if not his mate.

I never tire of the horned lark's courtship display. For one, it was early February and the horned lark was already thinking spring. And spring was still several severe snowstorms and many cold nights away. But the lark proclaimed spring long before the skunk cabbage's first little notation of the season, the peepers calling from the bog, colt's foot brightening the roadsides, and robins in the dooryard.

Horned larks are the first songbirds to nest here in the Midwest. One year, I found a horned lark's nest with three eggs at the end of March and showed it to a friend. A week later an April snowstorm (twenty inches) destroyed the nest. The cold and the destruction of their first clutch didn't deter the optimistic birds. They re-nested as soon as the snow was gone.

In favorable springs, newly fledged larks will be feeding in tilled fields by the latter part of April. Immature larks are great at confusing beginning birders – there is simply nothing in the field guide to match that nondescript bird feeding near the flock of American pipits … is it a longspur?

To me, the pair of horned larks' optimism is the hope and promise of spring. Whenever I come across the larks' well-hidden nest in the hayfield or pasture, I think of Barry Lopez' words in *Arctic Dreams*, "In a simple bow from the waist before the nest of the horned lark, you are able to stake your life, again, in what you dream."

I also remember when organic dairying was but a dream. In 1997, when a few of us of the "Where have all the flowers gone?" generation called a February meeting to order in our small farm shop to discuss what could be done to add value to our small-scale dairies and inspire a generation of young farmers, organic was on the front burner with the heat turned on high.

Around twenty farmers showed up. Sylvia Upp from OEFFA attended to offer her advice and help. (At that time Ohio had *no* certified organic dairy farms.) The Martins came and father Alvin shared the lumpy couch with our farm dog. The Schlabachs, Rob and the boys, were enthusiastic and eager for a new adventure. In spite of the skepticism expressed, about eight farmers, who already were believers in organic farming and living, were ready to roll. Mark Martin's farm was the only one certifiable at the time. The rest of us were a year or two away from certification.

Later that winter, Cecil Wright from Organic Valley came down for a meeting with us eight. Here is where our unfair advantage came in – Cecil's sister is Leah Miller, a former commissioner of our county. She now heads the Small Farm Institute and is very active in promoting pasture walks and sustainable and organic farming. Let's just say we had good connections.

A lot has transpired since that first meeting. Behind the original "let's go for it" group, there were about the same number of farmers that took a more cautious view before climbing on board, and then soon did. Off on the fringes there was the large "wait and see what happens; let someone else cut through the canebrakes" crowd and now most of those have become believers and are on board as organic producers.

In thirteen years, Ohio gained almost two hundred certified organic dairy farms. In that same period, the state's Director of Agriculture encouraged Dutch farmers to move to Ohio and establish multi-thousand-cow herds, many of which are now in financial difficulty. The Director was blind to what was taking place on his watch on a small scale. Our community alone added two thousand cows in organic and conventional grass-based dairies, but instead of one large operation like the Dutch dairies, those cows were supporting fifty families.

It wasn't until late 2002 that Leah Miller received a call from Cecil saying they wanted our milk. We were ready. When Fred took that first load down the driveway we cheered. At last, the dream had become reality.

Sometimes I'm asked if there is anything I'd do differently in going organic, if we had to do it over. Not really. For one, we weren't assured a market when we became certified, so there was no rush or pressure to reach a certain point. Since we produce over ninety-five percent of the feed for our forty-five to fifty-cow dairy and replacements, buying costly transition feed was never an issue. Our goal has always been to keep things as simple as possible. I read some Thoreau and everything Wendell Berry writes.

Since I'm on the soapbox, I'll hold forth for a bit longer. In speaking of simplicity in dairying, I'd like to say a few words on breeds of cows, and why we settled on Jerseys as the low-maintenance cow. Over the years, we had milked different breeds, but mostly the gentle fawn and whites from the Isle of Guernsey.

A wonderful cow, the Guernsey, milked by thousands of family farmers in the first half of the twentieth century. The cow did well for us, until she became primarily a show cow and classification became a must-do in registered herd circles. In order to win in shows and score high in classification, stature became number one. The Guernsey breeders did their job, and unfortunately the cow became tall and, in my opinion, frail and unenthusiastic grazers. We didn't want big cows, so we reluctantly bought our first Jersey.

Of the five major breeds of dairy cattle, the Jersey is the smallest. As its name implies, the Jersey hails from the British Channel Island of Jersey. The Channel Islands are off the French coast of Normandy. Victor Hugo spent many years in exile on the islands and there wrote *Les Misérables* and probably drank the rich and creamy milk of the Jersey.

For over two-hundred years, imports of foreign cattle into Jersey were forbidden, to preserve the purity of the breed. Before that law went into effect, cows had been given as dowry for inter-island marriages between Jersey and Guernsey. So in all likelihood the two breeds share some common blood.

Unlike the fawn and white Guernsey, the Jersey is often solid honey-brown, but can range in color from light tan to almost black with smokes in between and rarely broken with white. All purebred Jerseys have a lighter band around their muzzle, a dark switch (long hair on the end of the tail), and black hooves. The Jersey cows tend to be gentle and trusting, but the bulls can be as vicious and spiteful as any Spanish fighting bull. The rule is: always be cautious around a Jersey bull on pasture. My mother grew up with Jerseys and would tell us the story of Grandmother getting her ribs fractured by a playful young bull.

Besides being excellent grazers, Jerseys have three things going for them that I like — rich milk (4.8 percent butterfat; 3.8 percent protein), intelligence, and calving ease. This last merit is the key to longevity.

Our experience has been that a Jersey will freshen, get up, lick her calf, the calf nurses, the cow lies down and cleans. Simple.

Unlike with the other breeds, we always have a surplus of young stock to sell and that is a nice addition to the farm's income.

I could continue to pontificate on the merits of the Jersey and on selecting bulls from your own herd, but not now. Finally, turning over a family dairy to a daughter or son and their spouse that is thriving health-wise and financially, is extremely rewarding, as my wife and I have found out.

This was made possible because seven farmers from the beautiful hill country of southwestern Wisconsin had a dream and brought it to fruition. Now we too are living the dream.

Summer

One insect I find endlessly fascinating is the dragonfly. Yesterday while I was mowing hay, dragonflies-green darners, twelve-spotted skimmers, and a meadowhawk—were coursing over the top of the unmown clovers and grasses hunting for food. Hovering and wheeling, flying forward, backward, sideways, and straight up, each was done with ease and without apparent fear of being a quarter mile away from the nearest water in a field surrounded by insect-eating birds. Dragonflies have a certain hauteur that may intimidate birds into choosing slower food.

Ukrainian-born Igor Sikorsky must have observed the big green darner's skillful flight to come up with the idea and then building the first successful helicopter in the early 1940s. However, in comparison to the dragonfly's adept maneuverability, Sikorsky's machine seems clumsy, but it gets the job done.

Dragonflies are beneficial insects to have around the farm, although their value isn't as evident as that of the honeybees. Besides being a crucial pollinator of human food plants, it is the bees' end product that we savor – clover and black locust honey on the dinner table contribute greatly to our quality of life.

We lost our two colonies of bees over the winter. It is largely my fault, at least in losing our old and strong hive. They simply starved to death. I was so convinced that the black walnut sawdust treatment for varroa mites would work and carry the bees safely through the winter. In fact, it may have contributed to their starvation. The colony was free of mites and stronger than I had thought and thus consumed a lot more honey during the cold months.

Last year was an odd year for honey. Up through July, the bees made enough surplus honey that we extracted three gallons from the one hive. For the rest of the summer and fall, the bees barely kept even and entered the winter low in stores. I don't like to supplement-feed honeybees in the fall for their winter food source, but I should have.

The split and combined after-swarm colony starved, surrounded by honey. February 2010, as we all remember, was snowy and overcast with only five days of sunshine. It was not bitterly cold, but cold enough without the sun warming the hive that the bees didn't break cluster and move to honey. They also had very few days warm enough for "cleansing" flights.

As the days warm in late winter, bees will leave the hive, fly, and cleanse themselves, leaving brown streaks on the snow. Upon returning to the hive, they cluster around new stores of honey and eat well. I noticed the lack of flights in February and realized the bees were in trouble. But it was too late.

Now we have new bees; a three-pound package by mail from Texas and a five-hundred-pound log by boom truck. Sometime during the winter, the neighboring sawmill received a log that had a colony of bees in its hollow heart. They discovered it when the tree was being cut down to saw-log lengths and suddenly there were bees all around. Lee and David moved the bee log out of harm's way and covered the larger openings for winter protection. They offered the bees to me, and on a cold morning in early March, the bee log was moved to our farm.

The colony appeared rather weak and Lee thought they might be dead. But slowly they have built up into a strong colony of nice Italian honeybees. The hollow tree is filled with old dark comb and has obviously been occupied by bees for many years. My guess is that these light Italians swarmed and moved in last spring or summer.

The next step is to get ourselves a nice colony of bees from the log into a hive. I plan to use Sam Miller's method of using a bee-tight cone of plastic window screen with the large end surrounding the bee's entrance hole and directing the bees out of the log and into a spare hive box. Then I'll give the transferred colony a new queen, while leaving the old queen along with some of the young bees and sealed brood in the log so that they can build up into a strong colony before winter. I can't kill a good queen that carried her colony through a difficult winter. Ideally, and life is seldom ideal, the log bees will swarm and I'll be around to hive them. The hive box is ready. A swarm in June is worth a silver spoon.

(2010)

Fall

For the last week and a half I have been mowing pasture fields, roadsides, and odd little pieces that were put off for a more convenient time. That time is now here. The small-grain harvest is over and the last hay for the year is in the mow, and the corn isn't quite ready to be ensiled. We are in that period of not quite summer and not yet fall when work on the farm loses its urgency, at least for awhile, and my mowing is done mostly in the afternoons. And some days not at all. As Gene Logsdon would say, "It all depends ..."

The fields I am mowing are not the rotationally grazed ones but the permanent pastures—those interesting places along the creek and into coves shaded by the woods where tall ironweeds, wingstem, and joe-pye weed flourish. Places where the goldfinches nest and the dragonflies roam.

I have been told that I'm doing it merely for recreation or for cosmetic purposes. Perhaps for both reasons. But it is much more than that; it's downright therapeutic do be enveloped by air richly scented by cut mint and boneset and bee balm. With a sharpened knife in the sickle bar mower and a team that knows me as well as I know them, life doesn't get much better. We rest often in the shade of the sycamores, and while they switch the last flies of the year and the dog chases rabbits, I check out Salt Creek.

For over half a century I have been watching and charting the changes of the spring-fed creek, which has its headwaters near Mount Hope and Calmoutier and empties into the Killbuck Creek, north of Holmesville—the life within its waters and along its edges. Salt Creek is fast flowing; dropping nearly ten feet per mile, so naturally there are numerous riffles in its meandering course. When we travel from our farm to Holmesville, a distance of around eight miles, we cross Salt Creek nine times.

The changes in the waterway I've observed have been mostly negative. Gone are the smallmouth and rock bass, the black suckers and stonerollers. The first year of our marriage, my wife Elsie, who wasn't from a family of fisher persons, caught a fifteen-inch smallmouth in one of deeper holes. During their spawning season the bass would claim the better pools and send the other species – shiners and horned chubs mostly – packing. Dad had taught us boys to wait for a rain to muddy the waters and then drop a hook baited with a minnow into the pool and the bass was yours. It was so easy that we quit the practice because it didn't seem like fair chase.

Black suckers would only bite in early spring and then quit feeding on earthworms. The stonerollers, also in the sucker family, never bit. They would rest and likely feed, headed into the riffles and there remain motionless for hours unless spooked by someone or something, when they would quickly turn and shoot for the safety of the deeper water.

Also gone are the freshwater eels, those foot-long snake-like creatures that would be impossible to catch with your bare hands. We boys fully understood where the term "slippery as an eel" originated.

Likewise, the freshwater mussels have left the waters of our farm. In March and April, when the water was clear and cold, the single-footed track of the mussel could be seen on the silty bottoms of the slower moving stretches of the creek. Occasionally we would find a broken mussel shell along the edge where a raccoon had dined on the mollusk.

Not all is lost however; three new travelers have arrived in the last twenty years and now make the creek their home. One is the mink. During the Great Depression and the war years the sale of mink pelts put food on tables. For many years there simply were no mink around in this farming community. My brother caught one in the 1960s. Now the sleek animals are common and the muskrat has become rare. Mink feed on muskrats.

Another newcomer is the soft-shelled turtle. I saw the first one, actually a pair, two years ago. I have been told that the arrival of the softshell is not a good omen because they tend to inhabit poorer quality waters. A better sign is the tail feather of a wild turkey I found along the creek this summer. This is the first evidence of the big bird's return to our farm after an absence of over one-hundred-and-fifty years.

What has caused the decline of the life in the creek? There are a number of possible reasons and that includes channelization upstream, which tends to speed up the flow of water during heavy rains and thus fills in the fishing holes and tears out streamside vegetation and piles of driftwood. Agricultural practices have changed a great deal in the last five decades – more pesticide use, more livestock grazing on stream banks, and water drawdown during the summer months, especially in dry years, for irrigation have definitely contributed to the losses.

But all is not lost. While most of the changes have been in the waters of the creek, life along its edges remains rich in flora and fauna. Belted kingfishers and rough-winged swallows nest in burrows in the cutoff banks, dragonflies course the streamside, damselflies flit back and forth from stone to boneset, 'coon and deer tracks cross the sandbars, schools of minnows again swim in the shallow pools, the water flows clear and there are fewer algae blooms – and mowing in its presence remains pleasurable.

Now is the time to enjoy the autumn for the fullness it carries with it, love the trees until their leaves fall off, and then, on Thanksgiving Day, acknowledge our dependence.

(2010)

Home for the Holidays

One of the saddest days of the year for me is the summer solstice; the point where the suns ends its six month journey northward, pauses, and then begins its long trek south. I love the spring and its verdure: the strawberries and sweet cherries, and cultivating corn, and birdsong in the lengthening days of mid-June.

In July already, the first waxy red leaf of the black gum tree in the woodland whispers autumn, and by August the goldenrod confirms it. Summer's maturing and fall is approaching and sooner than I care to admit, so is winter.

Somewhere in the last few decades, the cold season of winter has lost some of its appeal for me. I still enjoy cutting firewood and then reading and resting embraced by the comfort of wood heat. I enjoy the barn chores, feeding and watching winter birds, and celebrating the holidays when food and talk is shared with family and friends and sometimes strangers.

For many generations in our community, a day of fasting and prayer was set aside after the corn harvest, in gratitude for the bountiful harvest. As rural people, we realized the fields were made fruitful by more than callused hands and sweat. The bounties of summer and autumn were stored in haymows, silos, corncribs, and granaries. The overflow of the gardens and orchards went into root cellars and barrels, and onto long shelves of mason jars filled with applesauce, peaches and pears, pickles, red beets, green and dried beans, corn and squash, tomato and grape juice, and sweet cider. All this in preparation for the winter months and this called for a day of thanksgiving.

Over time, this traditional harvest holy day merged with the national day of Thanksgiving, when the gathered family sits down to a meal that represents the culmination of the goodness of the year.

Almost every hand at our extended table had a part in the gathering of the bounty set before them. Everyone helped with the planting, hilling, weeding, bug picking, and digging of the Yukon Gold potatoes, now mashed and steaming from heaping bowls at each end of the table with lava-like flows of melted butter down its amber sides. Likewise for the corn—from the plowing, harrowing, and planting to the few shotgun blasts persuading grackles, cowbirds, and redwings to move on south (starlings we tolerate because they eat the Japanese beetles feeding on the silks of the corn).

Many times, we forego the more traditional turkey in preference of our own free-range Cornish-cross fryers. While my wife and I carried the feed and water to the broilers daily and penned them up each night to save them from predators, many hands helped on the birds' last day on Earth.

Next to the heaping platter of golden fried chicken is the dressing to accompany the potatoes, gravy to liberally cover both, sourdough bread and new honey. Cole slaw, sliced tomatoes and sweet peppers, mixed fruit from the farm, and cottage cheese pudding complete the menu.

Here is this family favorite—whip 2 cups of whipping cream, add ½ cup sugar, and 2 tsp. vanilla. Stir in 2 cartons of cottage cheese, then sprinkle ½ cup dry jello (more or less, any desired flavor; we prefer orange) over the cottage cheese mixture. Stir in well. Add three cups fruit. We like drained crushed pineapple and mandarin oranges.

My wife tends to alternate cottage cheese pudding with graham cracker pudding, which is another top-notch dessert. She will prepare the one for Thanksgiving and the other on Christmas. This dessert is simply a cooked and cooled cornstarch pudding put in layers with crushed graham crackers, whipped cream, and sliced bananas. Adding some whipped cream directly to the cooled pudding adds extra flavor, and probably a few calories.

After words of thanks from everyone from the youngest to the eldest around the table, the fruits of our summer and autumn's labor are savored. Last, but far from least, come the pies – apple from the Northern Spy and pumpkin topped with, what else? whipped cream. (I descend from a long line of Swiss dessert lovers; my grandfather supposedly never turned down a piece of pie in his life. It may have shortened his life. He died at ninety-two.) And of course, carafes of steaming, robust, shade-grown organic coffee finish off the dinner. The caffeine keeps us talking until the evening milking.

Then, in late December, we commemorate another rural event. In a stable, in a modest village in Judea, a child was born. The first to know were the shepherds in the night hills, who hurried to the stable and saw the baby lying in a manger. The faces of those humble sheep herders, men of no prominence in their religion or government, must have shone with wonderment as they hurried back to their flocks before the break of dawn.

Just as other families celebrate this obscure birth – a union of the holy and the secular – we do so with food, gifts in reverence to the innocence of children and a hope for humanity. Around our table, the dinner is similar to Thanksgiving Day, four weeks earlier. Instead of chicken, there will be baked ham; also candied sweet potatoes, cranberry salad, and assorted fruit pies or sometimes a variety of cheesecakes. The long table will have beeswax candles, in recognition of the thousands of little pollinators and makers of honey for our bread.

Christmas, as with Thanksgiving, is a day of gratitude for food, shelter, good land, and friends. Following just a few days after the winter solstice, it means a definite end to autumn and the growing season. Henceforth it is indoor time for the farm animals and for us.

Here, where the fires are burning good oak, I am having second thoughts over not particularly liking the winter season. After all, the sun is on its way north again and spring follows in due time. Winter? It is not bad at all.

LARKSONG FARM

1. Cliff Swallow colony
2. beehives
3. vegetable garden
4. fruit orchard
5. Elderberry bushes
6. Savannah Sparrows
7. Horned Larks
8. Red Fox den
9. Eastern Bluebird houses
10. Vesper Sparrows
11. fencerow of Black Cherry trees
12. Serviceberry grove
13. Shellbark Hickory trees
14. Great Horned Owl's nest
15. gigantic Northern Red Oak tree
16. Cardinal flowers
17. farm pond
18. Sugar Maple trees
19. old apple orchard
20. old Eshleman-farmstead foundation
21. American Chestnut tree
22. Red-tailed Hawk nest
23. Belted Kingfisher colonies
24. Northern Rough-winged Swallows

neighbor's land which we farm

Bobolink field

farm path

Larksong Farm

Harrier field

14

15

16

4

2

9

9

10

12

13

11

8

1

1

1

6

7

5

N

The Wooster Book Company is committed
to protecting the environment and to the re-
sponsible use of natural resources. The Wooster
Book Company is a member of the Green Press
Initiative, a nonprofit organization dedicated to
supporting publishers in their efforts to reduce
their use of fiber obtained from endangered
forests. *Letters from Larksong* is printed on 30%
post-consumer recycled paper that is manufactured through a chlorine-free process.

The Wooster Book Company works with
printers such as Thompson-Shore, Inc. that are
also members of the Green Press Initiative and
who help establish the chain-of-custody for this
initiative by supporting best practices developed by the Forest Stewardship Council.